sculptured
sandcast
candles

by GARY KOEPPEL

CHILTON BOOK COMPANY

sculptured sandcast candles

PHILADELPHIA   NEW YORK   LONDON

Copyright © 1972 by Gary Koeppel
First Edition   All Rights Reserved
Published in Philadelphia by Chilton Book Company
and simultaneously in Ontario, Canada,
by Thomas Nelson & Sons, Ltd.
Photographs by Brooke Elgie, Monterey, California
Designed by William E. Lickfield
Manufactured in the United States of America

Library of Congress Cataloging in Publication Data

Koeppel, Gary, 1938-
  Sculptured sandcast candles.

  1. Candles   2. Sand sculpture.   I. Title.
TT896.5.K64   745.59'3   72-8484
ISBN 0-8019-5748-6
ISBN 0-8019-5749-4 (pbk.)

for my mother and father,
whose working hands
are now mine.

acknowledgments

Bernard Malamud once said to me: "Books are written alone, on tables, in small rooms," to which, after writing this book, I should like to add, ". . . with a little help from your friends."

Davis McDaniel of the Monterey City Library for referring Bruce Andresen, of Chilton Book Company, to me;

John Milton and Crissie Persons, of Chilton, for their suggestions and patient attention to details;

Marguerite and Tony Staude who helped me to take time away from making candles so I could write about them;

Brooke Elgie for photographing the illustrations for this book with such care and clear eyes;

Paul Rollins, with help from Jim, Goph, Eliza, Tom, and Pepper, for operating the Coast Gallery during my absence, and for helping to make my absence even possible;

Lynn Montgomery for typing an immaculate copy from an almost undecipherable manuscript, and Little Lynn for being Keeper of the Candles while I was gone;

and finally, my thanks to Ripplewood, in whose cabin, beside the Big Sur River, I finally found solitude in a small room with a table, where I wrote this book.

For their part in discovering and making the candles, I would like to thank:

Susan, whose discarded tripod candle and $16.00 loan inspired my beginning, and Miriam, who encouraged me when I began;

Jan and Ruth, of the Tidepool Gallery in Malibu, who helped develop the refill concept;

the 7 candle helpers who worked with loving care in my Topanga studio;

and finally, special thanks to Sandy Goodman, who taught me that keeping a medium fresh keeps it alive, and to my Great Aunt Aud, who taught me love for the gifts of the sea.

Big Sur, 1972

contents

list of illustrations

color plates

sculptured
sandcast
candles

What you receive depends on what you give—

the workman gives the toil of his arm, his energy, his movement; for this the craft gives him a notion of the resistance of the material and its manner of reaction.

the artisan gives the craft his love; and to him the craft responds by making him one with his work.

but the craftsman gives the craft his passionate research into the laws of Nature which govern it; and the craft teaches him Wisdom.

—*de Lubicz**

*Baba Ram Dass, "Remember Be Here Now" (San Cristobal, N. M.: Lama Foundation, 1971; distributed by Crown Publishers, Inc., N. Y. C.).

CHAPTER 1

K the candler

MAGIC CANDLES AND THE SECRET CHEMICAL
IN THE SAND

Late one evening, while I was sculpting candles on location at Universal Studios' International Festival, a small, white-haired lady with sparkling eyes stepped from the ring of onlookers surrounding my sculpting stand and asked brightly, "Young man, how in the world do you make those candles?"

I was deeply engrossed in the candle I was sculpting, working quickly with the propane torch in one hand and a carving tool in the other, and so, without looking up, slowly replied, "Well, it's really quite simple. You dig a hole in the sand, pour in boiling hot wax, and when it cools and hardens, lift it from the sand, fill the depression in the top with wax, and wick it with a hot ice pick. Then heat up the sand-crusted sides with this torch, carve patterns into it with this tool, and you've got a sculptured sandcast candle."

She stood waiting as though there were more. After a moment, looking thoroughly perplexed, she asked if it were really that simple. I replied that basically it was a very simple process, then added that there were, of course, a few tricks. "Tricks?" she pondered. Then her eyes widened and sparkled again. "Oh," she intoned, and glancing around she leaned toward me and whispered, "You mean they're Magic Candles?"

She was so delightful I couldn't restrain myself from turning toward her, and with widening eyes I nodded, "yes." At this, she smiled knowingly, and with her new secret, disappeared into the crowd.

Magic, indeed! For the past five years I have sculpted candles on locations throughout California before audiences totaling over two million people. Among those whose questions I have tried to answer simply and directly, I have sensed a general awe and disbelief that the process of making my sculptured sandcast candles was as simple as I explained it to be.

On another occasion, while I was sculpting at the Disneyland Hotel Marina, a middle-aged gentleman, with a small boy, who had been watching me work for some time, finally ventured to ask me how I got so much sand to stick to the sides of the candle. He and his boy had tried making sand candles on the beach that very morning, he said, and they had failed miserably. Also, he asked, what did I use in the sand to make the finished exterior so hard?

I replied that getting a thick sand crust was a result of pouring boiling hot wax into a slightly damp mold. When poured, if either the sand was too wet or the wax too cool, the sand would not stick to the sides. To his second question I answered that the propane torches fused the sand and wax together—that the heat seemed to vitrify it, like glass, to the density of sandstone.

"But what do you mix with the sand?"

"Nothing."

"You mean it's just sand?"

"Well, it's beach sand."

He was hardly convinced.

"You mean you don't add anything . . . a chemical, maybe?"

"Really," I sighed, "it's only sand and wax."

"What about stearic acid?"

"It's pure sand, and pure wax." I concluded.

"Hey, Dad, how does he do that?" piped the boy. At this point the father took him in tow and replied excitedly as they were leaving, "It's a secret, Son, a secret chemical, and I think I know what it is!"

Time after time I found myself disbelieved, or at least suspected, for the simple truth seemed too difficult for most to accept. So I began answering questions with "The Great White Lie about the Secret Chemical in the Sand," or "The Sworn Oath of Trade Secrets passed down through generations of 'K' Family Olde-Guild Candlers," and yes, I even told some that these were Magic Candles made by me and my seven candle elves in a cave on a mountain by the sea. I am reasonably convinced that most people found the fantasies more credible than the facts.

Although I've explained a particular step or series of steps in the process of making my candles to virtually hundreds of people, I've never disclosed the entire process to any one person. I do so now because I want to share, in a sentence or paragraph, things that took me hundreds of hours to discover and comprehend.

I confide that I am extremely grateful for the opportunity to give back what was given to me, thus freeing me from being the only person who knows how to do this particular thing. Also, in the future, when someone asks me how I make my candles, I can reply, "Well, it's a very simple process, and it's described in complete detail on page so-and-so right here in this book." Now that, to me, is magic!

WHY PERMANENT, SCULPTURED, SANDCAST, DRIFTWOOD CANDLES?

I began making candles because I got fed up with buying candles that burned for only a short period of time before something went wrong—a drowned wick, a wick smoldered to an unlightable nubbin, a hole in the side spewing wax, to mention a few. Almost invariably, for one reason or another, the candles I bought went kaput! So I decided to make my own candles, candles that would be for burning.

Why sandcast candles? For some time I had been intrigued by an old, discarded, kaput sand candle (Fig. 1-1). Its squat, tripod shape and hard, black, sand exterior presented quite a mystery to me. Much of the rim had burned away, and the sand on the side was subtly stratified. Could it have been excavated from ancient ruins? I imagined it came from some prehistoric lava cave, and I could envision its flickering light illuminating primitive pictographs and crystalline stalactites within the cavern. Its possible history fascinated me, for it seemed as old as fire itself, but for me the deeper mystery lay in the process of how it had been made.

One night, after freeing the drowned wick in my kaput tripod candle with a twig of driftwood, I discovered that the flame of the candle not only illuminated the piece of wood, but also cast a moving shadow on the wall behind. I embedded the small piece of wood in the top of the candle and looked on thoughtfully. Feeling somewhat hypnotized by the flame, my eyes came to rest on the piece of driftwood, which looked like a miniature cypress tree. My mind meandered through my past to Heceta Head Lighthouse on the Oregon Coast, where I spent part of my summers as a boy with my great aunt and great uncle, the lighthouse keepers. From them I learned respect for the sea and love for its many gifts, especially driftwood.

From those boyhood days of beachcombing on Heceta Head Beach came my deep feelings and wonder for the wood that drifts ashore. Such a journey that wood makes! Washed from the forest by flooding rains and swept down waterways to float adrift in the sea, the wood is tumbled and scoured by the surf, then tossed ashore at high tide for bleaching in the sun. Driftwood—sculpture by nature, the greatest artist of them all. Why not mount it in a base of sandcast wax and position the wick to where it best illuminates the form? A sandcast driftwood candle! So I began.

I gathered driftwood and sand from the beach, bought wax and wick, scavenged a bucket and cardboard box, melted the wax on the kitchen stove, scooped a hole in the wet sand contained in the box, placed a piece of driftwood in the hole, and poured in some wax. I then laid a coat hanger across the sand mold and bent a length of wire wick into a candy cane shape, letting it dangle from the hanger into the pool of cooling, hardening wax.

The next morning, with classic Great Expectations, I pulled my first candle from the sandbox and, to my complete dismay, discovered that not one grain of sand had adhered to the sides. Moreover, the driftwood pulled loose in my hands, and the wick was badly kinked in a deep depression that had formed on the surface of the candle.

My disappointment slowly gave way to curiosity. Was the wax too cool when poured? Was the sand mold too damp? Why the large

4

1-1 "ancient" tripod sand candle

surface depression? How could the wick be kept straight? Would driftwood and wax adhere?

Then I had an idea, the Great Plastering Experiment. Using an old iron frying pan, I heated a mixture of dry sand and wax, stirred it into a bubbling hot, pasty goo, and with the zeal of an apprentice plasterer, proceeded to slap spoonfuls of hot goo onto the gleaming bald surface of my sandless cast candle. At first the goo melted vainly down the sides, but as it cooled and hardened, it became more manageable, then suddenly less so; I quickly borrowed a propane torch from a neighbor to heat it up. I must have plastered that poor candle for one entire evening with, of course, more of the goo adhering to me, my work table, and the side of the house than to the candle. The result was a quiet disgrace.

5

Yet, what I had learned! That plastering was indeed for the birds, and the propane torch was an incredible tool! Fire as a tool!

During the ensuing months I made three candles nearly every night, and with each candle, learned something new. Each exploration I ventured upon led to new discoveries which, in turn, opened new dimensions to explore. I learned how to place a piece of driftwood in the sand letting its shape determine the shape of the mold, how to position the wood (with as much surface exposed as possible) to form a strong bond with the cast wax, and how to make the driftwood and sand adhere so that the finished candle was a strong integral unit. In fact, I discovered how to embed the wood in the wax so well that I could lift the candle—even a 100-pounder—by the wood, without it pulling away from the wax. This was accomplished simply by lifting the wood out of the mold while the wax was still boiling inside, and then repositioning it, allowing the wax to flow behind and embrace the piece of wood.

I finally learned how to get a thick crust of sand, up to two inches, on the sides of the candle. I discovered that when the wax was poured piping hot into sand barely damp enough to support a molded shape, it actually boiled into and penetrated the sides of the sand mold. Once the casting had cooled and solidified, I found that a crust composed of wax-saturated sand had formed.

I also learned that after fan-drying all of the moisture from the crust, and then firing it with two propane torches, the wax and sand fused together and hardened to the density of sandstone (Fig. 1-2). In addition to making the exterior harder, this discovery eliminated one of the pesky problems of sandcandles: loose sand continually falling onto table tops (a condition I call "sandruff").

Then one day, while chopping up a stack of reject castings for remelt, I discovered two very important things that explained why some of my candles had been burning strangely. First I saw that in the center of each candle there was a core, an air pocket ranging in size from a golf ball to a tennis ball. I have since come to regard this as the "abominable air pocket," because it takes as many as three different fillings with wax, and a final check, to be certain that no air remains inside the pocket. That one flaw will cause an otherwise beautifully burning candle to suddenly flare up with a large flame that melts too much wax, too fast, from the sides, which floods the well and drowns the wick.

From the axed rejects I also discovered the problem of water in

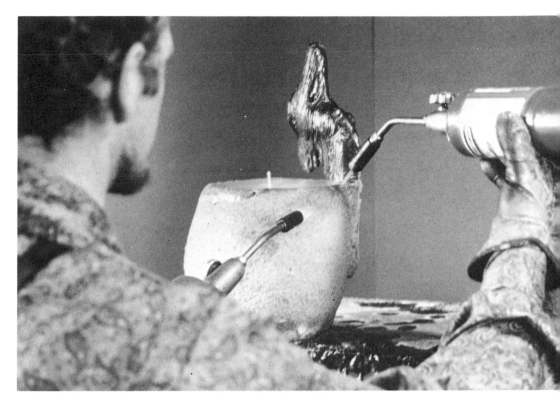

1-2　torch-firing the crust

the air pocket, a sad condition for a candle because it clearly pre-destines the wick to drowning-by-water. After a lot of nervous won-derment about how the water got inside the candle, I finally reasoned that, because wax expands when heated and contracts when cooled, and because the exterior of the candle cools first and the interior last, a vacuum forms in the center causing suction, thus drawing moisture from the bottom and sides of the sand mold. This also explained the depression which had occurred in the top surface of the candle, and which had kinked the dangling, candy cane wick.

My solutions to these problems were, again, incredibly simple. First, I found that as the candle cools and the top begins to depress, sticking an ice pick into the top and relieving the vacuum eliminates the "water in the air pocket" problem. Second, I learned how to fill the air pocket with wax (which I'll explain later in all of its abominable detail). Third, I discovered how and when to wick the candle. Thus ended three major problems with wicks that went kaput.

Then one evening, I discovered my first sculpting tool, an old-fashioned, long-handled, sharp-pointed, 5¢ can opener. With that, the idea of sculpting a sandcast driftwood candle was born. By heating the sand and wax exterior with the torch, I found that, with the can opener, I could more easily scrape through the crust to the pure wax beneath, and carve patterns that, almost as a bonus, came glowingly alive when the candle was lighted. I also discovered that, by using the torch while sculpting, not only was the carving made easier, but the fired exterior was made even harder than before.

As I continued experimenting and exploring, I slowly became aware that the driftwood was the key to the candle, because its size and shape determined the size and shape of the sand mold. From the mounted wood I got ideas of natural lines for sculpting patterns, and the grain of the wood inspired the type of texture to use on the candle. All this, I learned, came from the wood.

One of the first candles I carved (and felt good enough about to sign and keep) was shaped as a bowl with small stones and a piece of driftwood embedded in the side (Fig. 1-3). The carving and texturing were done with a torch and can opener, and the shape of the base somehow complemented the wood. I was beginning to learn something about the intangible balance between the wood, wax, and sand.

It all seemed finally to come together one day when I finished The Drummer (Fig. 1-4). The driftwood was exceptional, the drum-shaped base was nicely proportioned and had a respectable, if somewhat thin, crust, and the sculpting pattern, though more by accident than intent, was appropriately primitive. The Drummer is on permanent exhibit at the Tidepool Gallery in Malibu, and has been burning almost daily since its completion in 1969.

Before long, people began buying my candles, and everything was developing rather well until I learned that most people weren't burning them. They didn't want to ruin them, they argued, which was understandable, but they weren't even being lighted, and I had taken considerable time and care to make my candles for burning!

So I developed a refill, a 3 inch candle for inserting into the well which is burned out by the original wick. Initially, I made the refills in sand molds formed by organic apple juice jars, but they needed torching to remove the sand and that was too complicated. So I began using disposable, 10 ounce paper cups for molds.

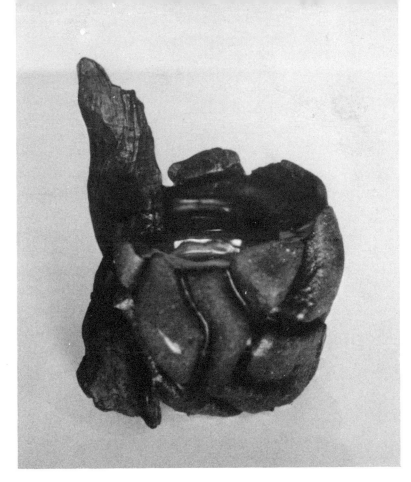

1-3
The Rock and Wood
Bowl

1-4
The Drummer

1-5
a beginner's first
sand candle

1-6
a beginner's first
driftwood candle

And that's the story of how I came to make a nearly kaput-proof, permanent, sculptured, sandcast, driftwood candle.

To illustrate the ease with which these candles can be made, I have pictured two candles which were made by beginners (Fig. 1-5, Fig. 1-6). Neither individual had any kind of instruction other than asking a few questions while watching me work in my studio. Their first candles so impressed me that I wanted to share them with you.

THIS BOOK

I should begin here by admitting that I have never read a book on making sandcast candles. In fact, it wasn't until I began writing this one that I even looked for books on this subject. Only then did I find that no material of any depth or detail was available. What I know, I have learned by doing, by making over 5,000 candles during the past five years. I know now that the best way to learn how to do something is by doing it alone, slowly, and step by patient step.

The main advantage of this book is that it will save you time, lots of time. I can describe in one paragraph what took hours, days, or even months for me to learn. If you seriously want to make 1 or 100 sculptured sandcast candles, this book will spare you virtually months of labor. That is quite an advantage considering that it takes a lot more work than talent to make sculptured sandcast candles.

The main disadvantage of this book is that it will deprive you of some of the explorations and discoveries that I experienced. Perhaps the saving grace here is that, given the basics, you will be freer to explore realms that I've just touched upon, or better, realms I haven't touched at all.

Now that you know something about me and my experience, I'll help you set up your studio and get started. I'll walk with you through the four basic steps of sandcasting and sculpting and then show you how to make 18 different candles, varying from "basic-shaped" sandcasts to sandcast driftwood and shell candles. The later chapters deal with making the refills, candle care, candles in candle holders, and finally, Chapter 13 divulges the last of my heretofore untraded "trade secrets," a list of supplies and suppliers.

CHAPTER 2

the home studio

KEEP IT SIMPLE

Five years ago I borrowed $16.00 to buy 100 pounds of wax and 10 yards of wicking. With no change left over, and little in the way of practical resources to draw upon, I had no choice but to keep it simple: to scavenge my equipment and invent my own tools. My first studio was an outdoor patio perched on the hillside of a Southern California canyon called Topanga. The kitchen was conveniently situated just inside the door where, on the electric range, I melted wax in 5 gallon buckets. My mold boxes were waxed cartons scrounged from the meat market, and my work counter was a sturdy old patio table.

As you prepare your studio, imagine yourself a pauper, regardless of how well-fixed you may be. In so doing, you will learn how

2-1 casting equipment

to make better candles, and you will discover, as I did, the nature of your own deeply-rooted inventiveness, natural self-discipline, and competence. If you are as much in need of these self-explorations as I apparently was, you will also learn something about the nature of such things as patience, humility, and gratitude.

Sand, wax, and wick; a bucket, burner, and box; that's all you really need to begin. However, a few well-chosen comments about the casting equipment, sculpting tools, and candle making materials might help you to make your beginning somewhat more graceful than mine was.

CASTING EQUIPMENT

Mold Box

During my first 2 years of sandcasting, I used waxed cardboard cartons and wooden crates lined with cardboard for my mold boxes.

Because it took so long to level the bottoms of candles cast in unevenly floored mold boxes, I finally built two large plywood boxes with flat surfaced flooring (Fig. 2-2). This step all but eliminated the tedious process of leveling. I also added removable lids that could function as work counters when the mold boxes were not in use.

I would suggest that, for now, you use either waxed cardboard cartons or wooden crates for your mold boxes, and then build your own once you discover what you need. Whichever you use, be sure to line the floor with a flat piece of wood.

Melt-Vat Burner

A gas burner is the fastest, most efficient, and most economical way to melt wax. I used an electric range for the first 3 years, and it was really quite sufficient for making a few, or even quite a few, candles, but a gas stove or custom gas burner is, simply, better.

Melt-Vat

Find a 5 gallon bucket with a sound bottom and a handle, and you'll have an excellent vat that will melt over 30 pounds of wax at one time. I still use my first vat, but now only as a pouring bucket for a spigotted, 55 gallon drum-vat (Fig. 2-3). If possible, it's a good idea to weld, or have welded, a reinforcing bead of metal around the seam at the bottom of the vat to insure that melting wax will not seep out, oxidize on the burner, and ignite.

Insulated Gloves

Always take precautions to protect yourself from being burned by the boiling wax. Heavy, insulated gloves should be kept close to the melt-vat and, without exception, used for any operation involving the handling of hot wax.

Relief Rod

If you melt down a vat of wax and don't use it all up, the left-over wax will cool and solidify. When the vat is reheated, the wax in the bottom will melt first and begin to expand. The force created by the expanding wax can easily burst the bottom of the vat. To prevent this, you should always stand a "relief rod," on end, in the vat of cooling wax. A wooden cane, a metal rod, or a broom handle, will each make an excellent relief rod. The rod should be slightly taller

2-2   my studio, with mold box in center

than the sides of the melt-vat so that it may be easily gripped for removal.

If you forget to use the relief rod, you will have to dig a relief hole, by hand, through the hardened wax to the bottom of the vat. If you do not do this, the bottom of the melt-vat will blow out when you reheat the wax, and cause a wax fire. With these possible disasters in mind, you will always remember to put in the rod when the wax is still soft and cooling and to pull out the rod when you begin to remelt the hardened wax. It is also very important for you to "ream out" the relief hole as the wax is melting, so that it will not plug itself up and cause a buildup of pressure.

Fan

When wax is heated it vaporizes, changing from a liquid to a gas. This vapor will cloud the air in a closed studio. A small fan will keep the working air fresh and hasten the drying of wet castings.

Oil Can

An oil can raided from your tool box makes an excellent container and dispenser for liquid scent, which is a flammable concentrate.

Oiler's Can

This prize junk store acquisition, with its elegantly long spout, functions remarkably well as an almost dripless pitcher for topping castings and pouring refills.

Pouring Pitcher

Rummage around for a container with a handle and a large opening at the top—a coffee pot, a milk pitcher, or a pan with a lip—which will be used for dipping hot wax out of the melt-vat and pouring it into the molds. The large opening allows the wax to pour smoothly and is useful for dipping wicks, and dip-filling refills.

Thermometer

Any thermometer that registers 350°F or over and is immersible, will do. A candy thermometer is perhaps best, for it has a 450°F scale and a clip for easy attachment to the melt-vat. An ordinary meat thermometer rigged with wire for suspension, will also work well.

Hatchet

With compliments to the boy scout pack stored in the attic, a hatchet will prove helpful in chopping up slabs of new wax as well as rejected wax-castings, though a hammer works almost as well.

Tongs

Conveniently available from your patio barbeque set, a pair of toothed tongs comes in handy for dipping driftwood and for fishing out lost thermometers and other objects dropped accidentally into the melt-vat.

Fire Extinguishers

Water will only spread, not extinguish, a wax fire. You should have at least 2 rechargeable chemical extinguishers, one near the melt-vat and another beside your sculpting table. Unfortunately, they last only for a few seconds and will not extinguish much of a fire. Consequently, I keep a large bucket of dry sand near the melt-vat because sand, when poured over a wax fire, smothers the flame and absorbs the liquid wax for easy cleanup. One caution, however: if sand is super-saturated with flaming hot wax, it can turn into a medium just like wicking and sustain a flame. So have on hand enough dry sand to completely cover a fire area.

Work Counter

Any reasonably stable table which will sustain the weight of several candles will do—an old kitchen or patio table, sawhorses and plywood—anything waist-high that provides surface area for preparing castings.

SCULPTING TOOLS

Finish Table

The only non-tool you will need for the sculpting process is a stand or tall table on which to sculpt. My first finish table was a plywood-covered chair mounted shoulder-high on top of my work counter and braced against the side wall of the house. Later, I paneled a wooden pallet and set it on concrete blocks stacked on top of my work counter. Finally, a friend and metal sculptor designed and built me a portable tripod stand, complete with a formica top and two propane torch holders (Fig. 2-5). I am still using that stand today.

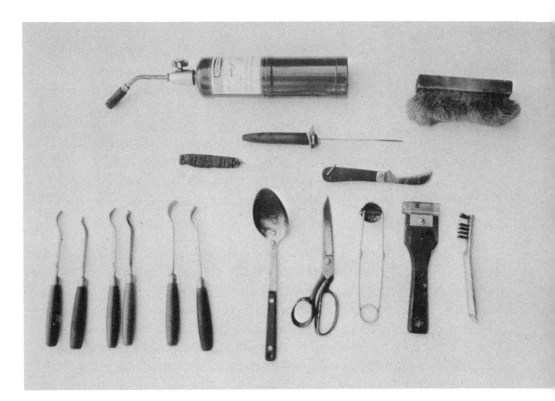

2-4   sculpting tools

2-5
portable finish table

Propane Torch

Besides the carving tool, the torch is the most useful tool in making sculptured sandcast candles. One torch can suffice, but there are occasions for using two different orifices, pinpoint torch and blow torch. These torches are often used simultaneously, as in firing, so I recommend having two torch heads, each fitted with a different orifice. You should check out your local fire regulations before beginning to work with the torch.

Small, refillable tanks are now perfected and available, as are larger tanks with the torch head mounted on a hose. I would strongly suggest your investing in the latter system, right off, especially if you plan to make more than a few candles, for the savings accumulate quickly. Compare prices with your local propane distributor and judge for yourself.

Brush

Almost any brush will remove loose sand from the side of the casting, but I've found that wallpaper brushes are cheap, readily available, and last a surprisingly long time.

Sticker

A multiple-use tool, the sticker is used to relieve suction in the casting, fill the air pocket, and wick the candle. A wooden or plastic handle is essential, either an ice pick or a ground-down screwdriver will do a good job.

Can Opener

My first sculpting tool now serves mainly for inscribing my initial in the bottoms of candles I like, but I still use it upon occasion for carving and texturing. Finding an old-fashioned can opener made with good steel and a long handle is becoming more difficult, but there are still some around waiting to be found. If you wrap electrician's tape around the shank of the can opener you won't burn your gloved fingers when torch-heating the tool for carving.

Linoleum Knife

For under $1.00, this tool, with its curved cutting edge, makes easy work of trimming castings, and can double as an occasional carving tool capable of cutting interesting patterns into candle crusts.

Wire Brush

Found in any paint or hardware store, the wire "toothbrush" is used solely for brush-texturing. The brush won't clog up with sand so easily if you extract the second row of bristles with a pair of pliers.

Scraper

A common paint scraper with replaceable edges is used with the torch for scraping and cleaning wax from surfaces, and especially for leveling and cleaning the bottoms of candles.

Striker

Sparks from the squeezed striker light the torch more easily than matches. A striker usually comes in the kit with the torch.

Scissors

For cutting and trimming the wick, any sharp pair of shears or scissors will do.

Spoon

Another discarded kitchen utensil, the spoon is used for sprinkling dye onto the wax filled molds and for spooning (not plastering!) a hot mortar mix of sand and wax into candle holder bases in which a candle is then mounted and fused.

Sculpting Glove

A thin buckskin glove should be worn on the hand holding the carving tool. Don't glove the hand holding the torch, it will only impede certain movements needed for sculpting.

Carving Tools

When I discovered Marples of England Wood Carving Tools and ground them for wax sculpting, my candles advanced considerably (Fig. 2-6). The shape of the "spoon-bit gouge" tool increased my choices in carving, making more patterns and greater precision possible; the wooden handle made the tool cooler and more comfortable to grip; and since Sheffield Steel is slightly better than can opener steel, the tools managed to stay sharper longer.

I see no reason why other makes of carving tools wouldn't work as well, as long as you find some with a similarly shaped spoon-bit gouge. I have included information in the last chapter about mail-

2-6　Marples tool before (left) and after (right) grinding

ordering these Marples gouges in the event that you cannot find them, or a substitute, locally.

Tool Sharpener

Whether you use a hand file, a stone, or an electric grinder, it is important to keep all of your tools as sharp as possible, for your work will then be more efficient and, therefore, more enjoyable.

Electric Drill

An optional tool most useful when fitted with a long-shanked ⅛ inch bit for drilling holes to relieve the air pocket. With a grinder attachment, it can double as a tool sharpener.

CANDLE MAKING MATERIALS

The three essential materials you will need are sand, wax, and wick; it is important to obtain the exact materials described below. Dye, scent, and felt pads are not essential materials and can be selected on the basis of personal preference. Driftwood and shells can be used or not, again depending on the type of sand candle you want to make.

Sand

Two of the most interesting discoveries I've made are that each beach contains a different size, type, and color of sand, and that, of the dozen different sands I've experimented with, only a few work well for both casting and sculpting. Try to find a sand composed of medium-sized granules evenly dispersed throughout; fine sand fuses poorly and makes for a soft finished exterior; sand containing large granules tends to complicate carving and to dull tools quickly. Settle for a medium-grained sand, fairly evenly dispersed with similarly sized granules, and you'll have a smooth, dense crust to carve.

The type of sand is as important as the size of granule. If at all possible use beach sand, but, if it is not available, river sand will do. Only if absolutely necessary should you use the washed and graded sands sold by sand and gravel companies, for the cleaning process—washing, then hot-tumble drying—removes the tiny microscopic grit and edges from the sand granules. Consequently, the washed sand and wax never knit strongly together, and so, while the crust is being sculpted, it sluffs readily and is difficult to control.

Wax

Modern language usage allows the words "wax" and "paraffin" to be used synonymously. At one time, wax referred only to natural substances such as beeswax and carnauba wax, but it now includes paraffin, which is actually a waste product distilled from a petroleum refining process.

During the past five years I have experimented with over a dozen different waxes varying in type, melting point, and degree of refinement. I've worked with beeswax, carnauba wax, most of the standard paraffins, and even a special high-melt, "computer-blended" experimental wax. The wax best suited for sandcasting and sculpting candles is called "154°-156° melt-point, highly-refined paraffin." I buy mine from Standard Oil of California in 2 ton lots.

The melting point and the degree of refinement are the only two things you need to know about to buy wax. The term "melting point" refers to the temperature at which a particular wax melts. As a general rule, the higher the melting point, the longer the candle will burn.

The term "degree of refinement" refers to the amount of petroleum oils still in the paraffin. The more highly refined the wax, the cleaner the candle will burn. Poorly refined, low melt-point paraffin is much easier to find than 154°-156° melt-point, highly-refined paraffin, but any extra effort you need to make to obtain this particular wax will be worth the results, for no substitute works quite as well.

Stearic acid is a hardening agent often added to soft, low melting point waxes, but it in no way improves the burning of the candle. In short, it's an additive you can nicely do without.

Finally, wax can be purchased in 11 pound slabs from hobby shops or in 110 pound cartons from petroleum distributors. You should shop around first, for like everything else, the more you buy the less it costs.

Wick

Wire wick is the best wicking for candles that burn an internal well. The wire supports the woven cotton and prevents the flame from drowning. Be sure to use size "large" because that size of wire burns a 3-4 inch diameter well into the center of the candle which, by sheer coincidence, just happens to contain a refill made in a 10 ounce paper cup.

Dye

By using only three colors of dye in my candles (golden yellow, orange, and dark brown) I can obtain an infinite number of tones, all of which are warm earth colors that relate well to the driftwood. Using crayons or packaged chunks of colored wax is costly and ineffective, and using food coloring won't work because it is water-soluble, not wax-soluble. Powdered, wax-soluble dyes work best and can be found in any candle supply store.

One word of caution: concentrated dyes are a toxic irritant to eyes and skin; they should be handled carefully and stored beyond the reach of children and animals.

Scent

If you want your candles pleasantly, as opposed to pungently, scented, I suggest that you buy only high-quality, concentrated liquid scent and use it sparingly. I use only jasmine, honeysuckle and bayberry, but scent is available in almost every fragrance.

A word of caution also applies to scent. In its concentrated form, it is highly flammable and should be stored in a metal dispenser; also, it can burn the skin and, if sniffed too closely, can damage nasal tissue (and the sense of smell).

Felt Pads

Although I call this one of the nonessential materials, felt pads are a thoughtful and appreciated finishing touch. Three 1 inch felt pads on the bottom of a candle can make people with fine furniture your friends for life.

Driftwood and Shells

If you want to make sandcast driftwood or shell candles, you will find beachcombing the most enjoyable part of the experience. If you live too far from the sea, wood from the forest or river bank is just as beautiful as driftwood, and the experience of gathering it just as relaxing and rewarding as combing a beach. Under no circumstances should you buy these natural gifts from suppliers, for in so doing you deny yourself an important experience and, somehow, lessen the integrity of the candle.

THINK SAFETY — THINK FIRE!

Wax in a solid or liquid state is, ironically, nonflammable; it will ignite only when in a gaseous state. You can demonstrate this by pouring melted wax in a can and firing it directly with torches. Wax will flame only when it is converted by heat from a solid, to a liquid, to a gas, then via the medium of a wick, ignited. To this there is only one exception, the "flash point"—the lowest temperature at which the wax will combust and ignite independent of a wick—the point at which its oxidizing gases will explode. If overheated wax in a melt-vat on a stove were to reach its flash point, the entire liquid mass would mushroom from the bucket, explode in mid-air, and like napalm, convert everything it touched—including skin—into a flaming wick. So take care and take heed: the flash point of 154°-156° melt-point paraffin is around 350° and under no circumstances should the temperature of the melting paraffin go over 300°. Remember this well, for it is the only major precaution you need to work safely with wax.

To summarize briefly the fire and safety measures to which I've previously alluded: keep at least one chemical fire extinguisher near your melt-vat and burner; if your burner is gas, surround it with firebrick and/or asbestos; if your burner is an electric range element, keep the surface area of the range wiped clean, and never lift off the melt-vat when the element is still red-hot; use insulated gloves while working around the melt-vat, and a thinner glove for sculpting; if possible, cover your work counters with formica or other fireproofed material, and keep everything burnable—from leaves to litter—picked up and stored in metal containers; finally, work slowly, with fire and safety foremost in your thoughts. Enjoy the making of your candles by keeping in mind the old truth that getting there is half the fun.

CHAPTER 3

making the mold

While photographing the illustrations for this book, the photographer, Brooke Elgie, revealed to me why railroad engineers always seemed to be happy people who smiled and waved to everyone. "Remember how as boys we all wanted to be railroad engineers?" he queried. "Well, they were the ones who got to be the engineers, and they're happy as hell about it!"

I feel the same way about making candles. It was a long time in coming, but I finally got back to my sandbox, and have enjoyed playing in it ever since. Perhaps you will share such a fate upon rediscovering your sandbox.

Let's now assume and imagine that you have gathered all of the necessary equipment, tools, and materials for making a sculptured sandcast candle—which has also necessarily included at least one excursion to the beach, river, or forest for gathering sand, wood, and shells—and you are ready to go to work. It begins, alone, in your sandbox.

PREPARING THE SAND

If the sand you've gathered seems full of rocks, glass, bottle caps, pop tops, or other such treasures, sift it through a window screen into the mold box. Once there, it needs to be leveled, moistened, and compacted before it can be molded.

Leveling

Fill the mold box with sand to a depth of about 8 inches and smooth out the surface. Level it well so that the finished mold won't be higher on one side than the other.

Testing the Moisture

Before actually wetting down the sand, test the amount of moisture already present by digging out a hole and feeling if the sand is dry, damp, or wet.

Moistening

Dry sand needs wetting, wet sand needs draining, and damp sand is just right for making molds.

If the sand is too dry, moisten it slowly and evenly with a fine-spray hose nozzle throughout the mold box—slowly and with occasional testing to avoid getting the sand too wet, and evenly so that no areas of powdery-dry or crumbly-dry sand remain. Dry sand will cause "landslides" which collapse the walls of the mold.

If the sand is too wet, poke or drill small holes in the floor of your mold box and wait for the excess water to drain out, then plug the holes with damp sand. If this excess water is not removed it will accumulate in the bottom of the mold box, flood your mold, and collapse the lower walls.

If the sand is nicely damp, it packs well with a squeeze of the hand, and the sides of a moisture-testing hole can be patted to firmness.

Compacting

With flattened hands pat the level, damp, sand throughout the mold box with an even, consistent motion, as though you are quietly beating a drum with both hands. Tamp around the edges of the mold box especially well. Compact the sand until it has changed from feeling spongy to feeling firm. The better your compaction, the more intricate and precise shape you'll be able to mold in the sand.

Water in the Mold

If you discover a pool of water forming in the bottom of an already made mold, simply pour in some dry sand and scoop it out when it has absorbed the water. Continue pouring in dry sand and scooping out wet sand until the floor of the mold is relatively dry. Some moisture in the bottom of the mold won't matter, but an excess amount will either collapse the lower walls or seep into the wax and ruin your candle.

THE BASIC-SHAPE MOLD

"Basic-shape" sand mold is the term I use to describe a simple, bowl-shaped hole which is the basis for every other candle shape it is possible to make in sand. With the thumb and middle finger, the basic bowl can be quickly transformed into an oval, triangle, square, five-point, etcetera. But, finger-sculpting and other techniques will be described later; for now, let's begin with making a basic sand mold.

Digging the Hole

With the sand now level, damp, and firmly compacted, stand directly over the mold area and, pretending that you are a crane operator and your hand a claw-bucket, slowly excavate a perfectly round, cylindrically-shaped hole in the sand, clear to the floor of the mold box. When you've cleaned most of the loose sand from the floor, step back and measure or eyeball the hole: the top should be about 5 inches in diameter and the sidewalls should be about 7 inches deep. If the hole doesn't suit you, fill it up and dig another.

Shaping the Walls

When you have mastered making the cylindrical hole, reach down into the hole about mid-way, and with the back of your slightly rounded hand, scrape sand from the sidewalls in a circular fashion and transform the straight walled cylinder into a concave bowl. You might think of yourself as a potter working in reverse—from the inside-out rather than from the outside-in.

3-1 measuring the basic-shape mold

Smoothing the Mold

Now that you have a roughly-turned bowl, work even more slowly and smooth the curved wall. Clean the loose sand from the inside upper rim and from the surface around the mold. Then scoop out most of the excess sand from the mold and, with the back of your hand, work the remaining sand into the floor of the mold, rounding the bottom.

The pictured basic sand mold measures 7 inches deep, 5 inches in diameter at the top and bottom rims, and 6 inches at the widest point in the curved sides (Fig. 3-1). These dimensions represent the minimum-size candle you can make for it to be "permanent," which means that it is large enough to burn a well which will contain a refill, without burning through the sides of the candle.

To summarize this process: a mold is made by digging, shaping, and smoothing out a hole dug in damp, compacted sand—and it's so. simple it can be done by an adult as well as a child!

THE DRIFTWOOD MOLD

Making a driftwood mold begins with the wood rather than with a preconceived shape. Always give the wood its due, place it thoughtfully and allow the shape of the mold to evolve from the shape of the wood.

Dipping the Wood

Salt from the sea removes the natural oils from the surface of the wood and the naturally-weathered finish somehow doesn't look good in a candle. Most wood finishes I've tried tend to plasticize and destroy the driftwood's natural qualities. So, holding the bone-dry wood with tongs, I dip it into a vat of wax heated to 225°. If the wax is much cooler, too much stays on the wood, and if much hotter, it burns and chars the wood. Dipping the wood in wax returns some of the oils the sea has sapped, and enhances the wood's color, grain, and texture.

Positioning the Wood

Study the wood carefully and discover what you see in it; turn it over and around and decide which part should be embedded in the wax (Fig. 3-2). Scoop out some sand and position the wood in the mold to best reveal what you saw. In the piece of wood pictured, I saw a small torso with an oval head and a large eye—a cyclops—and I knew that I wanted to position the wood so that its eye would stand out prominently when illuminated by the candle flame (Fig. 3-3).

Seating the Wood

When you have the wood positioned where you want it, seat it by packing sand firmly around it, both front and back (Fig. 3-4). Then, using your finger-tips, tamp the wood snugly into place.

Making the Mold

With the wood now well positioned and firmly seated, you are ready to shape the base. Work from the wood forward; determine

3-2
The Cyclops
—studying the
driftwood form

3-3   The Cyclops—positioning the wood

3-4
The Cyclops
—seating the wood

3-5
The Cyclops
—the finished
driftwood mold

where the wick would best illuminate the wood (which is also the center of the candle), and then begin to work outward until you've formed something resembling a bowl shape. Keeping one eye on the wood, dig the hole, shape the walls, and smooth the mold.

A basic-shape mold evolved for the driftwood cyclops, and I remember wondering, as I finished the mold, how the finished candle would look with a flame-like pattern carved in the base with a can opener (Fig. 3-5).

THE SHELL MOLD

The only difference between making a shell mold and a driftwood mold lies in the procedure of seating the shell by deep undercutting in the mold. In preparing the mold for these two types of candles, the shape and size of the mold should be inspired by, and evolve from, the shell and the wood. The mold, it should be remembered, becomes the candle base on which these natural sculptures are mounted. The sculptured sandcast base is simply a pedestal and the candle flame a light source.

Undercutting in the Mold

After the shell has been positioned in the sand and seated firmly in place, carefully remove it and, using the index finger as a knife, cut a deep groove under the "seat" (Fig. 3-6). Then reposition the shell and tamp it securely back into place. This procedure strengthens the bond between the shell and wax by exposing more area for each material to adhere to the other, forming an extremely durable **bond**.

3-6
The Melon Shell
—undercutting in
the mold

33

CHAPTER 4

casting the wax

Casting wax into the finished molds should be done with extreme care to avoid serious burns. Insulated gloves should be worn at all times, and the molten wax should be poured in a direction away from where you are standing.

POURING

When the wax has been heated to a temperature ranging from 250° to 275° (the hotter the wax, the thicker the crust), it is ready to be poured into the sand molds. Whether you ladle the wax from the melt-vat with a pouring pitcher, or pour it directly from the vat, be sure the gas or electric burner is turned off before you begin. Wax will oxidize and ignite if spilled on a flaming gas burner or red-hot electric element.

4-1 wax cast at 250°

Pour the hot wax slowly (aiming well so more wax ends up inside than outside the mold) and you will discover the sights and sounds of sand casting—a churning-bubbling-hissing-steaming as the wax boils out the moisture in the mold and boils into the sand (Fig. 4-1). As soon as the boiling action has settled down, you will see that the level of wax in the mold has receded below the top surface; a considerable volume of wax has penetrated the sand and the mold should be filled again with wax. In about ten minutes, after the wax has contracted from cooling, the mold will need "topping"— the final filling with wax.

If you want to obtain an extremely thick crust on the casting, heat the wax to its limit, 300°—but not one degree hotter! When poured, you'll immediately discover the difference between 250° and

300° wax: instead of churning and boiling, the 300° wax fairly rumbles in the mold, foaming and smoking like lava in a volcanic hole (Fig. 4-2). Because of the super-expanded volume of 300° wax, the mold requires much more wax for topping and the casting takes much longer to cool before it can be removed.

RESETTING WOOD AND SHELL

The simple secret of casting wood or shells with wax lies in the technique of resetting. As soon as the wax has been poured, lift the wood or shell carefully from its seating, then reimmerse it in the wax and position it for the final time (Fig. 4-3).

Resetting allows the wax to flow behind the wood or shell and saturate the sand in the "seat." This procedure creates a bond so strong that the cooled casting—weighing up to 100 pounds or more —can be lifted up by the wood without separating.

TOPPING

Five to ten minutes after the initial pouring and first filling, the wax in the mold will have contracted enough to need topping up. To top the mold, pour either 250° or 300° wax into it, filling it to the rim (Fig. 4-4). This is an especially important step for driftwood and shell candles, for the wax will have contracted two or three inches below the top of the mold, when solidified. If the mold is not topped, a critical portion of the shell or wood, which should be immersed in wax for maximum binding and strength, will be exposed.

SCENTING

Scent is activated by a flame and its main function is to compensate for the odor of the burning cotton wick. If you want a fragrance to permeate your candle, including the crust, you can add scent to the wax before pouring, while still in the melt-vat. This, however, is somewhat wasteful and unnecessary, for much of the scent will evaporate from the vat, and a scented, sand crust will never emit much fragrance.

If you want scent throughout the wax, add it after the mold has been poured and topped (Fig. 4-5). Don't wait too long after that, for the wax must be hot enough to dissolve and disperse the liquid scent; if the wax is too cool, the scent will "freeze" and fall in frosted

4-2   wax cast at 300°

4-3
The Melon Shell
—resetting
the shell

4-4
topping the mold

4-5   scenting

lumps to the floor of the mold. If this occurs, torch-heat the top surface of the cooling wax until it is hot enough to dissolve the scent.

DYEING

Dyeing, like scenting, must be done during a critical period in the cooling stage of the casting. The wax must be calm and cooling in the mold, and must already have been topped so that the colors will not be stirred around and homogenized. Yet, the wax must be hot enough to dissolve the powdered dyes. Test for this by sprinkling a small amount of dye into a mold and observing the reaction: if the wax is moving around or still too hot, the powder will quickly dissolve and disperse throughout the mold; if the wax is too cool, the powder will sit on the surface film of the wax and must then be dissolved by torch-heating. But if the wax is within the critical temperature range, the powder will dissolve in the clear, hot liquid, tiny streamlets of color will descend majestically to the bottom, and it might occur to you to wonder for a moment about the nature of that particular magic (Fig. 4-6). Proceed by sprinkling very small amounts of different colors in separate areas around the top of the mold. (Although paraffin becomes clear when heated, it is pure white when solidified, so if you want a white candle, you needn't use any dye.)

Much of the living beauty of a sculptured candle is the glow that emanates through the carving. Consequently, the lighter the color of the dyes used, the more light the candle will emit when burning. Therefore, I tend to put the darker dyes (orange and brown) around the outside of the mold and the lighter colors (such as golden yellow) in the center where the wick will be. For dramatic color contrast, powdered dyes can be fused with a torch into the carved patterns of a nearly finished candle. This "staining" technique will be described in Chapter 6.

RELIEVING THE AIR POCKET

As the cooling wax in the mold begins to solidify, it continues to contract and creates an air pocket in the center of the cast and a depression on the top of the cast. At this point, poke a small hole in the center of the depression with the sticker to relieve the vacuum forming inside (Fig. 4-7). This is an important step, for if the casting is not "stuck" the force of suction in the unrelieved vacuum will pucker the bottom of the candle and draw water inside.

4-6   dyeing

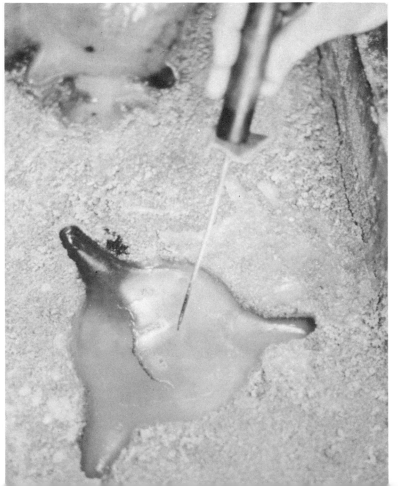

4-7
relieving the
air pocket

Because most of the casting procedures need to be executed during a critical period somewhere between not-too-hot and not-too-cool, your sense of timing will be challenged. Therefore, it will be helpful for you to remember and understand the sequence of the steps in casting, before you begin. After pouring the wax, the wood or shell must be reset immediately; as the wax contracts, the mold is topped up; scent the wax in the mold when it's still fuming hot, and dye it when the pool has calmed and cooled; then, when the surface hardens and depresses, relieve the poor, but nonetheless abominable, air pocket. In short, the old saw, "timing is all," applies anew.

CHAPTER 5

preparing the cast

Preparing the cast is the only part of the entire sandcasting process that even closely resembles work. This is so primarily because of the now infamous, abominable air pocket (the problematical nature of which will be exposed and resolved herein). The steps involved in cast preparation are as follows: after the casting is pulled, brushed, trimmed, and dried, it is brushed again and the top is torch-cleaned; fill-holes are then drilled or poked in the top, and the exposed air pocket is filled with wax; the air pocket must be drilled and filled again after the first fill-wax has cooled; finally, the casting is safety-wicked, and then it is ready for sculpting.

PULLING THE MOLDS

Pulling the molds is the first step in preparing the cast for sculpting and is the first opportunity for you to see what your hands have done. Study the casting well and see what you can learn from the experience of making its mold.

5-1
pulling the
mold

After the casted sand molds have cooled and solidified they must remain in the mold box for 12-18 hours, depending on the temperature at which they were poured. If removed prematurely, the shock incurred by the sudden change in temperature will cause the castings to crack, and they will then have to be scrapped for remelt. The test for determining when castings can be safely removed from the mold is, simply, to feel the top of one, then excavate and feel the bottom. If either surface is warm, repack the sand around the casting and wait until it has cooled. Peel the splattered wax from the sand around the castings and remove it all from the mold box, before pulling the cooled molds. When making molds, accumulated fragments of wax in the sand become a nuisance.

To extract a 250° sand mold casting from the sand, get a fingertip grip around the upper rim and pop it loose—usually by pulling, sometimes by pushing, and only rarely by digging out the sand and having to forcefully knock it loose (Fig. 5-1). Driftwood molds must be removed more carefully. I usually grasp hold of the wood and tug it gently to see how tightly the casting has adhered to the bottom of the mold box. If it cracks loose easily, I pull it out of the mold by using the wood as a handle, which is, incidentally, an excellent test for how well the wood and wax have bonded. If you suddenly find yourself holding the wood in your hand as the sandcast base lands on your toes, scrap the casting for remelt without a moment's hesitation, figure out what you did wrong, and make another mold. Shell molds must be pulled more carefully than driftwood molds not only because they are a more fragile material, but also because they don't bond as strongly with wax. So, scoop out some sand and pull on the base, not the shell.

If you find it difficult to remove a 300° casting, dig out the sand to the floor of the mold box, slide an L-shaped crowbar under the bottom edge, tap it lightly with a hammer, pull back on the bar and, thanks to leverage, pop the casting loose.

Next, using a wallpaper brush, brush off the excess wet sand, which is clinging to the sides of the casting. Then, trim the rim with a sharp linoleum knife (Fig. 5-2), and place the casting upside down in front of a fan.

CLEANING THE CAST

After the casting has been drying in front of a fan for about 24 hours (or longer without the fan) test its dryness by firing a small section of the crust with a torch; if any moisture is still there, you will hear the water sputtering from the heat, so let it dry longer. When the crust is completely dry, brush off all of the loose sand, and then turn the casting on its side and torch-clean the top (Fig. 5-3).

If the floor of your mold box was not flat, you may have to level the bottom of the casting by using the torch and scraper. This can be a ticklish maneuver (I've often spent more time leveling the casting than sculpting it), but the bottom of the casting must be both flat and level. So, take the time to do it now, if needed, and you will discover the sheer beauty of a perfectly flat and level floor lining the bottom of your mold box!

FILLING THE AIR POCKET

Here's where you learn why I've been calling the mysterious air pocket abominable. Using either a red-hot sticker or an electric drill

5-2
trimming the
cast

5-3   torch cleaning the top

with a long, thin-shanked bit, punch or drill 3 or 4 "fill-holes" in a 3 inch diameter circle around the center of the casting; make sure the holes pierce the air pocket. But beware, for forcing the tool—sticker or drill—can, will, and does crack the casting. Therefore, in making holes to pierce the pocket, always stick with a red-hot sticker or drill slowly with a sharp bit.

Next, heat some wax for filling to 250°, put it in a pitcher that pours well, mix in scent if desired, and add the appropriate dye to match the color of the casting. Now take the torch and with the pin-point flame, melt the wax around the fill-holes until they open freely into the air pocket. Then, with the torch in one hand and the pitcher in the other, fire the flame toward the air pocket and slowly pour in the fill-wax, all the while torching the cooler outside circumference of the fill-wax as it rises and fills the air pocket (Fig. 5-4).

When the air pocket has been filled and the level of fill-wax begins to rise into the depression area, pour the wax even more slowly and torch the outer ring of rising wax hotter. Continue filling and torch-fusing until the top of the casting is full of hot wax. If the fill-wax is not hot enough or is not torch-fused in hotly enough, it will harden as a plate which will separate from the surface of the casting.

After several hours, this first filling of wax will have cooled, contracted, and, yes, left another air pocket in its center. The good news is that it's somewhat smaller than the first air pocket. So, repeat the entire process: drill or hot-punch 3 or 4 new fill-holes, fuse in the second filling of wax, and then let it cool and harden (Fig. 5-5).

At this point, the air pocket may or may not be filled. If you have doubts, drill and test for air, but usually two fillings suffice. Besides, the air pocket will be poked once more near the end of the sculpting process.

If you are not now convinced that the innocent looking air pocket is actually an abominable problem, may I suggest your waiting to pass final judgment until the wick of your favorite, most beautiful sculptured sandcast candle one day goes mysteriously kaput —then form your own opinion about the infamous, overworked air pocket.

SAFETY-WICKING

"Safety-wicking" is the term I use to refer to a technique of wicking a candle so that if by accident it is ever left burning and unattended for a long period of time, the wick will burn down its well to about

5-4
filling the
air pocket

5-5   removing bubbles from the air pocket

2 inches from the bottom and, because of the melted pool of wax beneath the flame, the end of the wick will lose its footing, keel over, and drown in the pool of liquid wax. Please note that this is not a foolproof method of making a candle perfectly safe; there are no methods for that. A burning candle should be treated exactly as a burning candle—with enough respect for flame to never leave it unattended for any long period of time.

Preparing the Wick

Take a length of large-size wire wick, hold it against the side of the casting about 1½ inches from the bottom, and cut it about 1 inch above the top surface of the casting. Next, dip the wick into an open topped pitcher filled with 200°-225° wax. With the thumb and forefinger, strip off the excess wax while it is still warm. Then, as it cools and hardens, roll the flared ends and straighten the wick into a taut rod.

Usually, when a candle is first lit, at least half of the dry cotton wick burns and smokes away before it begins to draw up and burn the melting wax. Dipping the wick in wax presaturates it and prevents it from burning down to a nubbin when lit for the first time.

Inserting the Wick

Either the red-hot sticker or the long drill bit can be used to make a wick-hole in the surface of the casting. Whichever tool is used, take a moment to make the hole in the exact center (remember that the burned-out well will measure 3-4 inches in diameter). Drill or hot-punch the hole straight down, stopping about 1½ inches from the bottom (the point at which the spent wick will keel over and drown). Knowing exactly where to stop is the essence of safety-wicking, and is an easily solved problem. Hold the drilling tool vertically against the outside of the casting and, with the other hand, hold a straight tool in a horizontal position about 1½ inches from the bottom (Fig. 5-6). Then, touch the tools together in a perpendicular position, and make a careful visual note of where the shaft needs to stop to reach the proper depth.

It is important to drill the hole absolutely straight down. If the hole is angled, the wick will be angled, and the well it burns out will be lopsided. Now, forewarned, drill or hot-punch the wick-hole slowly, keeping the tool straight from side-to-side and from front-to-back.

48

brush-texturing

grooving

finished Basic-Shape Candles

*(from left to right,
top to bottom)*

The Starfish
The Seven-Point Star
The Five-Point Star
The Oval
The Double Mantle
The Six-Point Star
The Stump
The Stone Bowl
The Square
The Triangle

finished Shell and Stone Candles

The Melon and Stone
The Three Piece Abalone
The Conch

(from left to right, top to bottom)

The Bark Bowl
The Unicorn
The Wood-Flame
The Cyclops
Casper

finished Sandcast Driftwood Candles

chain and manzanita candle holder

mirrored redwood candle holder

tripod candle holder

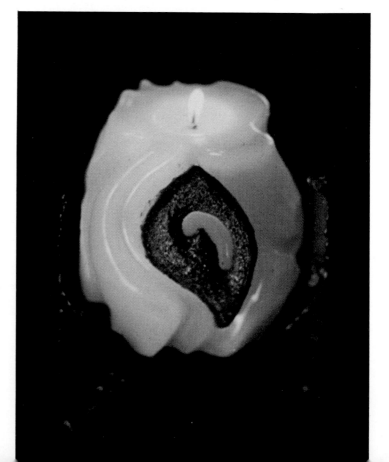

5-6 measuring for the wick-hole

Next, take the stiff, waxed, wire wick "rod" and insert it into the wick-hole, making certain that it goes all the way down (1½ inches from the bottom of the candle). Finally, with a pinpoint torch, fuse in the wax around the wick and smooth out the entire top surface (Fig. 5-7).

With the air pocket filled and the wick inserted, instead of a casting, you now have a candle—a sandcast candle ready to be sculpted.

49

5-7
torch-fusing
the wicked
candle

50

CHAPTER 6

*sculpting
the
candle*

But among all the arts,
I know of none more hazardous,
none less certain of the outcome
and consequently more noble,
than those which call
for the use of Fire.—*Paul Valéry**

Discovering the propane torch and the can opener as interdependent carving tools made me poignantly aware of my hands, of their dexterous ability to shape and mold a physical thing, and of their power to create something never before touched or touched upon. From sculpting with these tools, I also learned to appreciate the fact that my hands were a pair which, when working together in a single, coordinated movement—the torch in one and the tool in the other—could transform a crusty mass of sandcast wax into an object of beauty. The more I sculpted the easier it became to fire the crust to lava and scrape it away. Finally my hands were so attuned to the

---

*"Degas, Manet, Morisot," trans. David Paul (1960), *Vol. 12* in *The Collected Works of Paul Valéry*, ed. Jackson Mathews (Paris: Editions Gallimard; London: Routledge & Kegan Paul Ltd. and Bollingen Foundation; Princeton: Princeton University Press).

torch and tool that the pinpoint flame of the torch seemed to jet from an orifice in the tip of my forefinger and the carving tool seemed to become a curved, steel fingernail.

One evening, after a long day of sculpting, I paused and stood looking at the palms of my hands. My whole body began tingling with sensations—from forearm to shoulder, and up and down my spine—and I began to realize that my hands held all, that everything was there, and I felt grateful tears form in my eyes for having been able to become one who earns his way with his hands. Even today, when my overactive mind gets tangled, all I need for untangling is to slip on my glove, take torch and tool in hand, and begin sculpting a candle.

BASIC SCULPTING STEPS—THE STONE BOWL

Sculpting the candle begins with "firing" the crust, the hot crust is then carved with the torch and spoon-bit gouge, after which the surface of the sculpted pattern is textured and glazed. The air pocket is then hot-punched for a last check, the grooves are cleaned and glazed, and the finishing touches are applied. Remember to keep the torch orifices clean (for a hot flame) and the tool sharp (for easy cutting) for these small efforts will make the difference between enjoying your work and working to enjoy it.

Firing

First, place the casting on the finish table and, for the third time, brush the loose sand from the crust. Then, torch-dust and scrape the bottom clean and torch off any sand or accumulated dirt on the top surface, taking care not to ignite the wick. Using two torches if you have them, one a blow torch and the other a pinpoint orifice, evenly heat the entire surface of the crust, which will darken as the wax melts around the sand granules. Melt in all of the excess wax around the top rim, but avoid "over-firing," for burning too much wax out of the sand will cause sandruff and a weakly bonded crust. When over-firing occurs, the sand chars, smokes, and spurts in hot granules from the overheated area. These granules have a morbid affinity for eyes, so be careful.

Carving

Position the candle upright on the finish table, with about an inch extending over the edge, so that the carving tool can pass from the

6-1   The Stone Bowl—the first cut

top to the bottom of the crust without striking the table. While the crust is still hot from firing, torch-heat the tool and study the shape and surface of the candle. As with making a mold, rather than fixing a pattern in your mind, it is both more exciting and more natural to allow the pattern to evolve from the shape and surface of the crust.

The first cut is the most important. By allowing the curvature of the surface to inspire a line, draw the line with your eye, heat it with the flame tip, and then score it by slowly drawing the tool through the heated crust (Fig. 6-1). Once the line is scored, torch the groove and scrape away the sand, improving and refining the line as you go. Continue heating and scraping until the tool has cut completely through the crust and has peeled a ribbon of pure wax from the groove.

Turn the candle, position it for the second cut, and proceed in the same manner. Visualize the line, preheat it, then score and scrape

6-2 The Stone Bowl—the second cut

through the crust to the wax (Fig. 6-2). Allow the lines to evolve slowly, and complete one before moving to the next.

As you move slowly around the candle, regardless of how few or how many cuts you make, you will eventually come to the area where only one cut remains. Examine and resolve that area carefully, making sure that the last line relates to, and connects with, the first line you cut (Fig. 6-3).

Now that all of the lines have been cut, let the candle cool until the crust has hardened again. Then place the candle on its side in the front right-hand corner of the finish table with the top surface extending forward beyond the edge. With the torch flame barely touching the wax area between the wick and the lower edge of the overhanging candle, melt off all of the sand that splattered on the top

6-3   The Stone Bowl—resolving the last cut

during the cutting. Then turn the candle upright and fuse in any wax
that splattered on the sides while cleaning the top.

Texturing

With the carving design now roughed out, the candle is ready
to texture. After studying the pattern, determine which type of texture will be most suitable: smooth, raked, brushed, or dappled. These
textures will be described later, within the context of appropriate
examples. However, don't limit yourself to these, as there are many
more textures awaiting discovery.

For the round candle illustrated I decided upon a smooth texture
because I imagined the candle to be a stone bowl. I proceeded as follows: with the edge of the carving tool, I first scraped off and then

6-4   The Stone Bowl—edging to obtain smooth-texture

rounded out the jagged edges of the cuts until they became smoothly contoured with the surface of each sculptured pattern; completing one edge of a pattern before moving to the next, I worked around the candle until all of the cuts were smooth (Fig. 6-4).

Glazing

Reduce the flame of the torch to a fine pinpoint and carefully torch each pattern of the design between the cuts, from top to bottom (Fig. 6-5). The intense heat will draw wax to the surface which, when cooled, will firmly seal in the sand and leave a glazed finish on the carved and textured crust.

Hot-Punching

This is the final check on the air pocket to determine whether or not any air still remains in the center of the candle. Heat the sticker point red-hot, then poke it into the top of the candle an inch or so from the wick (Fig. 6-6). If an air pocket is still present, you will feel it give way when you pierce its chamber. Remove the sticker at once, flame the hole briefly with a small pinpoint torch, and then plunge the sticker in and out until no more bubbles issue from the hole. Make another hot-punched hole directly across from the first and repeat the operation.

Torch the top smooth, taking care not to push melted wax over the edge onto the finished sides. More often than not, wax does spill

6-6   The Stone Bowl—hot-punching the air pocket

over and drip down the sides, usually into the grooves. This problem is resolved in the next step which, for more than one reason, I've named grooving.

Grooving

The procedures of texturing, glazing, and hot-punching have splattered sand into the grooves since they were first roughly cut. At this point, all of the sculpted grooves must be cleaned with a fine flame point and a heated tool.

Proceed by heating a groove slowly, from the bottom to the top, without making the wax run. As the flame, in slow motion, passes beyond the top edge, draw the tool through the groove and scoop away the splatter in a quick, even, easy-does-it motion. As you draw the tool through the groove, the torch should be following an inch behind to glaze and heat the groove for a second cut. With this cut you peel off a curling ribbon of clean wax with the torch following in glazing pursuit (Fig. 6-7). Groove and glaze all of the cuts in the candle to ready it for the finishing touches.

Finishing Touches

While waiting for the outside to cool, use a pinpoint torch to smooth out the dimples now formed in the top from the earlier hot-punching, and while the wick is still warm, straighten it and pull it taut.

As soon as the candle is cool enough to be placed safely on its side, lay it down on the finish table with the bottom extending an inch or so over the edge. With the torch and scraper, heat and clean the bottom. It is a good idea at this point to check the level of the bottom of the candle by standing it upright. If it tilts or rocks, push it back and forth with enough downward force to leave scratch marks on the high points. Then lay the candle on its side and, using the torch and scraper, level off the scratch marks. Test it again, and repeat the above procedure until the candle is level.

Now, glaze the bottom surface and apply 3 self-adhesive, 1 inch felt pads. Stand the candle on a clean surface, and retorch any areas marred by the leveling and cleaning procedures.

Trimming the wick is an important finishing touch, for it can determine whether or not your sculptured sandcast candle will be permanent, that is, take refills. The wick should be trimmed ½ inch above the surface of the wax. If it is trimmed shorter, the flame will

6-7   The Stone Bowl—grooving

burn out a well too small to contain a refill, and if it is left longer, the flame will burn too large and will melt through the sides of a minimum-size candle. So, one-half of one inch, ok?

This completes the sculpting which turns a basic-shape casting into a Stone Bowl Candle (see color insert). Because this will be the only description of all of the basic steps of sculpting, let me reiterate the process: the crust is fired and then carved with a torch and tool; the carving is then textured, and the texture glaze-fired; hot-punched, smoothed, and grooved, the candle then gets the finishing touches of cleaning the bottom, felt padding, and trimming the wick.

To conclude this chapter on basic sculpting steps, it seems appropriate to describe how to sculpt with a can opener.

6-8 The Cyclops cast

CARVING WITH A CAN OPENER — THE CYCLOPS

Having followed the evolution of the Cyclops candle from its creature conception while studying the wood, to the making of its basic-shape bowl mold, you may recall the image that I preconceived and described—if its one eye was illuminated by the candle flame, and if its base was sculpted in a flame pattern, the Cyclops would almost come alive on a firebowl pedestal.

The flame pattern is best obtained by carving and rake-texturing with a can opener. The specific techniques featured in the description of the carving of the Cyclops will be scoring, the first cuts, rake-texturing, grooving, and finishing.

Before cutting into a driftwood candle, study the wood and base

6-9 The Cyclops—scoring the line

as you are firing the crust. When the crust is fired, turn the candle toward you and, without thinking, begin cutting the first line.

Scoring

With the thumb positioned on the back of the can opener and the torch directly beneath the V-shaped can opener gouge, slowly draw the tool down the side scoring a line that curves with the contour of the candle base (Fig. 6-9). Making several passes with the torch and tool, continue scraping until reaching the solid wax. Scoring the line before cutting makes the carving line easier to control.

First Cuts

My first cut into the Cyclops began in the front-center and angled conspicuously parallel to the head and sloping shoulder of

6-10   The Cyclops—rake-texturing

the mounted creature. As with the Stone Bowl, the first cut determined how all of the following cuts would be angled. I made a second
cut slightly to the left, freeing, between the two cuts, the first slender
flame-like pattern, a model for the rest.

Texturing

With the tip of the pinpoint torch and the point of the V-shaped
gouge, scratch rough lines into the heated surface with quick movements (Fig. 6-10). These lines should follow the curvature of the

established pattern. If the crust is overheated, the molten sand will run and the rough, raked-texture won't be obtained.

Grooving

Grooving with a can opener is accomplished in the same manner as with a wood carving gouge, and varies only in that the tool tends to smooth out the texturing on the outsides of the patterns where they border on the grooves. Rerake any edges accidentally smoothed when grooving, then glaze the surface, hot-punch the air pocket, and finish the candle.

Finishing

Instead of laying a driftwood candle on its cooled side for finishing, pick it up by the wood and while holding it in mid-air, heat, level, and glaze the bottom. If the wood is properly embedded in the base, it will not separate. If it does come loose, scrap the candle and review the entire procedure for setting the wood.

The Cyclops now needs only a flame to complete its reincarnation as a one-eyed creature hunched beside a bowl of fire (see color insert).

CHAPTER 7

specific sandcast candles

While the number of possible sand candle shapes is, virtually, unlimited, there are certain basic shapes that lend themselves to a variety of carving styles and textures. This chapter will describe how to make the molds for these shapes and will illustrate some of the various sculpting patterns and textures possible. The general processes of making the mold, casting the wax, preparing the cast, and sculpting the candle have been described in their respective chapters and will not be repeated here, for I recall having learned that repetition is monotonous and brevity is a blessed thing.

The shapes of the 9 candles illustrated in the following pages were all developed from the basic-shape mold, that simple bowl of a hole. Also, please note that there are many different sculpting patterns possible for any given shape. I begin the sculpting of each of these basic-shape candles by torch-firing the crust and scraping all

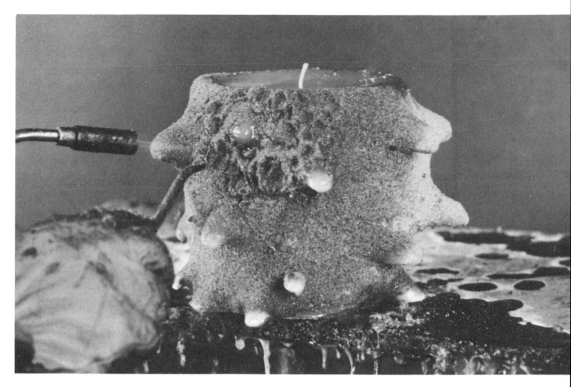

7-1 The Stump—dapple-texturing

of the sand from the molded protrusions or points, leaving the exposed wax clean and smooth. This procedure serves to accentuate the points, and thus highlight the candles' shapes.

THE STUMP

Mold Making

Make a basic-shape hole and, with the middle fingers of one hand, make indentations in the walls of the hole as deep as your knuckle. When indenting the upper part of the mold place your other hand flat against the top surface of the sand for support.

Sculpting and Texturing

As you torch-fire the crust, use the tool edge to scrape the sand from the protrusions, but don't melt them to nubbins. Then, torching and turning the candle once again, tap-tap the back of the tool against the surface and dapple-texture the lava-hot crust (Fig. 7-1).

7-2　The Stump—staining

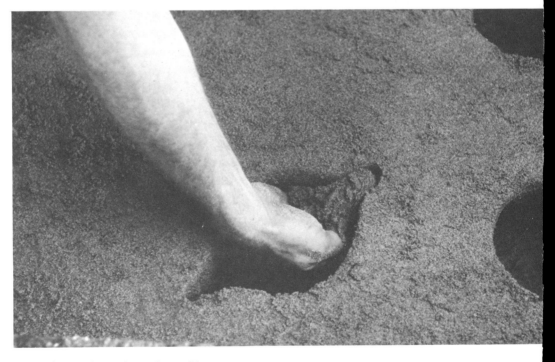

7-3　The Oval—making the mold

Staining

Dip your slightly warm carving tool into a can of dark brown powder dye. After a moment the powder will melt to liquid around the tool and then slowly harden on its surface. Position the dye encrusted tool against the candle and barely touch it with the flaming torch tip (Fig. 7-2). Then, with the torch only, fuse in the dye well and discover painting with a torch.

The stump candle can finish looking like many different things —bumps, warts, knobs, teats—but to me it's still the scorched stump of a burned out redwood tree.

THE OVAL

Mold Making

When you have a nicely bowled basic-shape hole, use your thumb to push a groove down one side and then scoop out the groove with three fingers. Then, thumb another, deeper groove, and remove the sand with a three-fingered scoop. Now, repeat this procedure directly across from the first impression (Fig. 7-3). Then, smooth and contour the grooves and sides.

Sculpting

The first pair of cuts begins at the edge of each protrusion. Curve each cut in toward the center and then down (Fig. 7-4). The

7-4   The Oval—the first cuts

second pair of cuts is made parallel to, and outside of, the first pair. These 2 cuts begin at the same point as the first pair of cuts, and end at the bottom of the candle, outside of the first cuts. The fifth and sixth cuts are angular. They begin at the top of the candle and join in the center, above the first pair of cuts, leaving a small triangular segment of crust in the upper part.

Texturing

For a tight dapple-texture, tamp down all the patterns, beginning with the uppermost portions and working downward, and clean out the grooves as you move from one area to the next.

Hence, her majesty, the Oval Queen.

THE TRIANGLE

Mold Making

Make a well rounded, potbellied basic-shape mold, and use the same technique to sand-sculpt the 3 points as was used for the Oval —use the thumb to push down a groove and three fingers to scoop out the sand.

Sculpting

The first cut is made by drawing the tool from the upper left-hand corner in an angular direction across to the center of the side, and then down to the lower right-hand corner. The second cut bisects the upper segment of the crust with an arch that begins in the upper center and joins the end point of the first cut (Fig. 7-5). The third cut begins in the upper left-hand corner next to the beginning of the first cut, and angles downward to join with the end point of the first and second cuts.

Texturing

The graceful angular lines cut in the Triangle are best accentuated with a brush-texture. Work from the upper segments downward to avoid splattering finished segments. Using your wire brush, stroke until a grainy appearance is achieved. Then, with the corner-tip of bristles, score deep strokes into the center of each pattern.

Pattern Variations

The Arch Pattern. Beginning in the center of one triangular surface, carve three arches with six cuts, then brush stroke for texture (Fig. 7-6).

7-5   The Triangle—sculpting the angular pattern

7-6   The Triangle—sculpting the arch pattern

7-7 The Triangle—sculpting the "V" pattern

7-8 The Square—making the mold

The "V" Pattern. Make 2 straight-line cuts, one from the upper left-hand corner and one from the upper right-hand corner (Fig. 7-7). Join them at the bottom center, thus dividing the surface into 3 triangular areas. In the next 6 cuts, carve a "V," with 2 strokes, in each segment. Then, edge the cuts with the tool and smooth the surface for a plain texture.

Note that the 3 patterns described are but a few of the number possible, and that each of these patterns can be used on other candle shapes, too.

THE SQUARE

Mold Making

The square mold also begins with the round, basic-shape hole. The corners are made by depressing the sand with the thumb, and the sand is scooped out with the index and middle fingers, giving the needed wide corners (Fig. 7-8). After the corners have been grooved, look directly down into the hole and rim the top edge with a finger tip. Then, smooth out the inside walls between the corners.

Sculpting

Using the torch and the flat edge of the tool, scrape off all of the sand on the end of each corner, leaving the exposed wax smooth (Fig. 7-9).

7-9
The Square
—cleaning the corners

To obtain the illustrated pattern, cut 2 vertical lines, from top to bottom, on each of the 4 sides. The lines should be spaced so that each side is divided into 3 equal segments.

The "X" pattern also works well with a square candle. Cut 2 diagonal lines on each side, one going from the upper left-hand corner to the lower right-hand corner, and the other from the upper right-hand corner to the lower left-hand corner. The 2 lines should cross in the center, thus forming an "X."

Texturing

Brush strokes will accentuate the pattern made by the vertical cuts, though a dappled or raked surface would also be effective (Fig. 7-10).

For the "X" pattern, brushing or raking would be tricky to execute. A dappled texture seems to complement this pattern best, though a plain surface might also work well.

THE FIVE-POINT STAR

Mold Making

Beginning with a basic-shape mold, use your thumb to score five grooves around the inside of the hole. Use only the middle finger to scoop the sand up through the grooves and out of the mold. Dig the grooves deeper, for more prominent protrusions, by using the back of an extended middle finger. Scoop out the bottom carefully, so as not to collapse the delicate edges of the five grooves.

Sculpting

Scrape all of the sand off of each point from top to bottom. Then, on the surface between each 2 points, make 2 cuts which meet at the top and bottom, forming a diamond shaped pattern (Fig. 7-11). One word of caution here—to avoid cutting too deeply into the base, angle the cuts slightly outward, toward the points.

Texturing

Vertically brush stroke the sides, and score an oval design on the diamond-shaped center pattern, with the edge of the brush.

The finished candle is a five-point, diamond star.

7-10
The Square
—brush-texturing

7-11   The Five-Point Star—sculpting

7-12   The Starfish—making the mold

7-13
The Starfish
—sculpting

THE STARFISH

Mold Making

The starfish should begin with a wider basic-shape mold than usual, one having a 7 inch rather than a 5 inch diameter. With the back of the index finger, slowly and carefully score the well compacted sides with a sloping, curved groove, keeping in mind the shape of a starfish (Fig. 7-12).

Sculpting

Scrape the five curved protrusions clean. Following the shape of the five curved points, make an angular first cut and a curved second cut between each two points. Join the cuts at the top and bottom so that a graceful pattern is formed between them (Fig. 7-13).

Texturing

Brush stroking best complements the sloping, curved pattern, and brush scoring all three segments on each side further accentuates the effect. When the candle is lit, the patterns glow and the Starfish almost seems to come alive.

THE SIX-POINT STAR

Mold Making

In a well compacted basic-shape mold, thumb-score 6 equally spaced grooves around the hole. Then, with the back of the middle finger, push downward to deepen and clear out the grooves. When cleaning out the mold work slowly to avoid collapsing any of the delicate points.

Sculpting

An "S" curve somehow accentuates the "sixness" of the mold shape. This curve is formed with a single cut that begins in the upper right-hand corner, curves toward, and turns at the center, and ends in the middle at the bottom (Fig. 7-14). Cut this curve into the surfaces between the 6 points.

7-14
The Six-Point Star
—sculpting

7-15
The Seven-Point Star
mold

Texturing

Using the wire brush, stroke the pattern in a curved motion paralleling the cut. Brush score deeper curved lines in the surface for further accentuation, if desired.

The Six-Point Star makes an excellent sitting or hanging candle.

THE SEVEN-POINT STAR

Mold Making

The seven-point mold is the most difficult of this type to make because it requires well compacted sand and considerable patience. Depress the thumb to score the seven grooves, and then deepen each groove with the middle finger. Looking directly into the mold from above, clean the top, sides, and bottom of each point (Fig. 7-15).

Sculpting

Scrape each point, from top to bottom, down to the wax. With the largest carving tool you have, cut a single vertical line into each surface between the seven points (Fig. 7-16). Begin the cut one inch from the top and end it one inch from the bottom.

7-16
The Seven-Point Star
—sculpting

77

7-17　The Double Mantle—making the mold

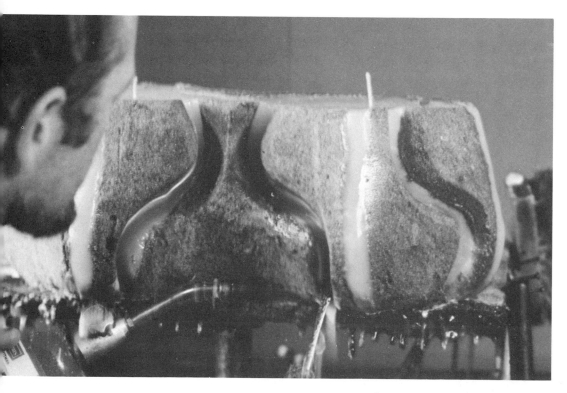

7-18　The Double Mantle—the first cuts

Texturing

After edging the rough cuts with the side of the tool, vertically brush and contour each surface, leaving a long window in each side. After finishing the seventh surface, take a rest.

THE DOUBLE MANTLE

Mold Making

With both hands dig two basic-shape holes in the sand, about four inches apart. When these holes are roughed out, push down with the thumbs on the area between the holes, thus opening a channel between them clear to the bottom of the mold box. Next, clean out the excess sand, contour the channel walls with the sides of the adjoining holes, and smooth out the inside walls of the mold. Then, with the thumb pushing downward and the middle finger scooping upward, make three grooves in each well in order to form a shape that resembles 2 square candles joined at one corner (Fig. 7-17).

Sculpting

First, using a scraper or tool edge, clean the sand from the six protrusions.

The first pair of cuts forms an hourglass shape which begins in the center of the bridge and curves to the inside bottom of the first protrusion (Fig. 7-18). The second pair of cuts bisects the segments on either end, between the points of the squares. The third pair of cuts is inside the patterns formed by the previous cuts (Fig. 7-19).

7-19 The Double Mantle—the internal cut

Texturing

When all of the cuts have been edged, round off the corners with the brush, stroking in line with the curvature of the patterns. Then, clean the grooves and rebrush any texturing that was scraped flat by the grooving.

This concludes the chapter on the mold making and sculpting of specific, basic-shape, sand candles. The finished candles are all pictured in the color insert. Practice with these and use the illustrated mold making procedures and sculpting techniques as a point of departure for your own explorations and discoveries.

CHAPTER 8

specific sandcast driftwood candles

It all begins with a piece of wood that snags your eye on the beach, in the forest, or on a river bank. As you pick it up, turn it slowly and look at it from every angle to decide whether or not it is sufficiently unique to warrant mounting in a sculptured sandcast wax pedestal. After packing it home (I've gotten many a curious glance when leaving a beach with a paratrooper's pack filled to overflowing with gnarled sticks of wood), wash it, to remove the salt, and dry it thoroughly, to prepare it for dipping in wax.

The Sandcast Driftwood Candle differs from the basic-shape sandcast candle in two important ways—in making the mold, and in sculpting the candle. Both of these differences occur because of the wood.

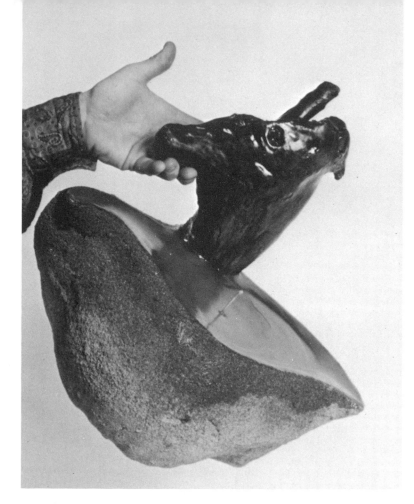

8-1 The Unicorn cast

Mold Making

The mold evolves from the shape of the wood rather than from a preconceived shape, even though the finished mold may often be a basic-shape. The wood is positioned in the sand first, then the mold is dug and shaped with the wood in mind.

Sculpting

The carving pattern executed and the type of texture chosen are both inspired by the wood. When first cutting the candle, let the lines develop to complement the general shape of, and the specific lines in, the wood. Use a texture on the carved patterns that complements and accentuates the texture on the surface of the wood. For example,

82

brush-texture to achieve a wood grain effect or dapple-texture to achieve a resemblance to bark.

In the following pages I have selected 4 driftwood candles for illustration. I have named each candle after something its piece of driftwood resembles—The Unicorn, Casper, The Wood-Flame, The Bark Bowl. The finished candles are pictured in the color insert.

THE UNICORN

Mold Making

I can describe how I made The Unicorn's mold, but I cannot explain why. After seeing the shape of a unicorn in the driftwood, I placed it in the sand and dug out a large basic-shape hole. I slowly began to "slice" curved grooves on either side of the hole with the flattened back of my hand. I hand cut the sand groove to the depth of the entire length of my fingers. From a top view, the hole was shaped like a head with 2 long curved horns. I'm certain, however, that any number of mold shapes would have made suitable pedestals for this noble creature.

The major procedures and techniques for sculpting a sandcast driftwood candle are described in considerable detail by the following example, The Unicorn. Keep in mind that all of the general steps for sculpting are described in Chapter 6 and will not be repeated here.

Cleaning the Wood

Sneak up on The Unicorn from behind and, with torch and tool, clean the casting slag, consisting of hardened sand and wax, from the back portion of the wood. Use the torch carefully to prevent burning the wood, and use a brush to remove the last sand particles.

Cleaning the Tips

With torch and tool edge, scrape all of the sand from the tips of the 2 curved horns.

Sculpting

First Cuts. Begin each of the first cuts at the curved area near the inside front tips of both horn protrusions. Carve a groove curving down from the top, toward the center, and continuing to the bottom (Fig. 8-2).

8-2   The Unicorn—the first cut

8-3
The Unicorn
—the second cuts

Second Cuts. The second pair of cuts bisects the upper segment and curves toward, and joins at, the center (Fig. 8-3). These two pairs of cuts closely resemble those of the Oval.

Third Cuts. Beginning in the tops of the grooves made by the first pair of cuts, carve each of the third cuts downward, parallel to the edge of the horn protrusion. Then, curve each line toward the center to join with the ends of the first pair of cuts, at the bottom.

Internal Cuts. Internal cuts are those cuts made inside of a larger carved pattern. In The Unicorn, the segment of crust left between the first and second cuts is wide enough to allow an internal cut—in this example, the eyes (Fig. 8-4). The eyes are best cut with a small, pinpoint torch tip and a very sharp tool. The line should follow the contour of cuts one and two, and the cut should be kept completely inside the segment.

Texturing

With torch and brush, stroke the carved designs until smooth. Remember to begin at the top of the candle and work down in order to avoid sand splatter on finished areas.

Glazing the Sand

Glazing an intricately carved and textured pattern can be tricky. If the material is overheated, either the wax melts and drips, or the lava hot crust slides and falls—both on nearly finished work. Therefore, glaze such candles slowly, with a tiny, pinpoint torch tip.

8-4   The Unicorn—the internal cut

8-5   The Unicorn—staining the sides

8-6
The Unicorn
—glazing the wood

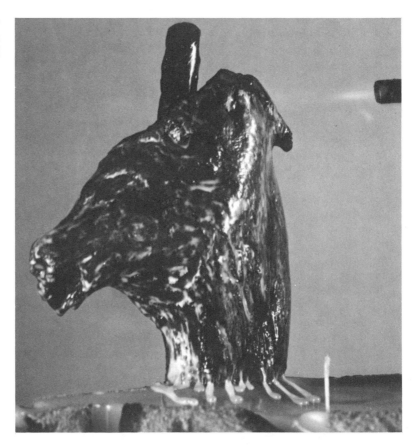

Hot-Punching

A word of caution here—if the punch is not hot enough when you check the air pocket for the final time, or if you exert too much force to make the hole, the pressure will crack the candle. So, don't cold-punch with a heavy hand.

Grooving

When grooving the center segment, or brow of the eyes, in the pattern, heat and groove the areas carefully to prevent losing the sand from the pattern directly below. Peel out the left groove and let it hang, then peel the right groove and turn the tool at the very tip of the "V," snipping off both peelings of wax.

Staining the Sides

With the torch, melt a small amount of a dark powder dye in a carving tool. Touch the dye encrusted tool against that part of the pattern to be stained and fuse-melt the area until the wax glaze completely absorbs the dye (Fig. 8-5). If dye isn't fused properly, it will come off when cool and stain anything which comes into contact with it.

Glazing the Wood

After hot-punching, use the torch, on the front of the wood, to melt off the excess wax remaining from the wax dipping procedure (Fig 8-6). You will often find that the melted excess wax flows, in streamlets, down from the wood onto the top of the candle. Fuse the streamlets into the top surface before they cool.

Glaze-Staining the Top

Smooth and torch-glaze the top surface of the candle, then add tiny droplets of dye and fuse them in (Fig. 8-7). If you have ever wanted to paint some day, do it now by spreading and swirling melted dye, on the top surface, with the flaming torch tip.

Finger-Grooving

If some wax happened to drip down into the stained grooves, while you were melting, smoothing, and staining the top, use your finger to wipe it out, then reglaze the wax in that area.

8-7   The Unicorn—glaze-staining the top

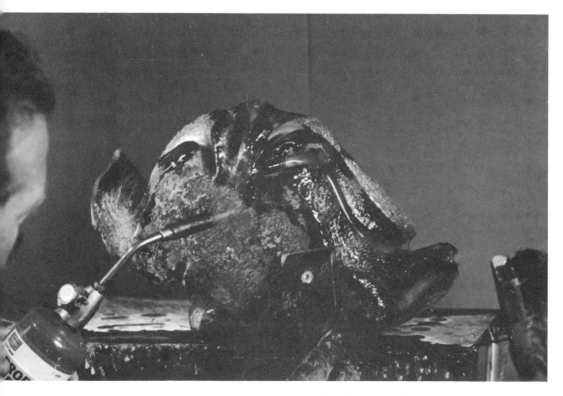

8-8   The Unicorn—fusing stain into the bottom

Cleaning the Bottom

When cleaning the bottom of a candle that has been stained, be certain to completely fuse and glaze the surface (Fig. 8-8). Table tops and other furniture can be permanently stained by candle dyes.

Signing the Work

I sign all the candles I like by inscribing my initial on the otherwise finished bottom, with my trusty 5¢ can opener. Any carving tool will do, but the "V" shape cutting edge does have the advantage of making a thin, accurate cut.

CASPER

Casper began with a piece of rotted and very weathered Oregon maple driftwood. The wood had three apertures: two that looked like eyes, and one that was an open "whooing" mouth. The top of the creature's head even looked like the pointed tip of a sheet. Slightly spooky looking, the wood resembled a ghost, so I named it after a friendly one.

Mold Making

The mold for Casper's pedestal evolved into a triangular form, scooped deeply at the bottoms of the three corners with the corners themselves grooved on an angle rather than straight up and down (Fig. 8-9). These angular grooves were formed by "slicing" the cuts with the back edge of the hand to the depth of the length of the fingers.

8-9
Casper—
making the mold

89

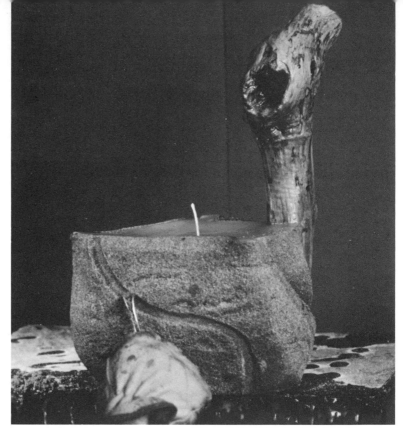

8-10
Casper—
the first cut

Sculpting

Following the general lines of the three angular corner protrusions, cut a curved groove in each side beginning at the top edge of one corner and sloping gently toward the bottom edge of the opposite corner (Fig. 8-10).

After the main cuts have been completed, make internal cuts on the patterns. First, score the line with the brush to facilitate the cut, and then cut out the grooves with a carving tool (Fig. 8-11).

THE WOOD-FLAME

I named this candle The Wood-Flame because the broad and thin piece of weathered driftwood I used had the form of a large, licking flame.

Mold Making

As with The Double Mantle, this mold begins with two basic-shape holes, but in this case a piece of wood is embedded in the channel and the holes are left rounded. Be sure to make the channel broad and wide enough to support the two sides, and to "bowl-out" both of the holes so that the grooves can be carved deeply (Fig. 8-12).

90

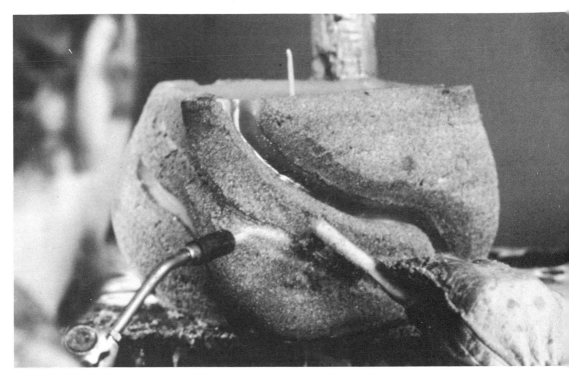

8-11   Casper—brush-scoring the second cut

8-12
The Wood-Flame
mold

8-13
The Wood-Flame
—the first and
second cuts

8-14
The Bark Bowl
—making the mold

Sculpting

Always make the first cuts in a driftwood candle in harmony with the shape of the wood, your basic inspiration. Note that the first two cuts in The Wood-Flame Candle were made by following the contour of the left and right sides of the wood, making the subsequently freed pattern a direct imitation of the wood's shape (Fig. 8-13). The rest of the cuts followed the contour of the candle's surface.

THE BARK BOWL

The Bark Bowl represents one of my favorite candle styles. It was designed originally as a hanging driftwood candle. Because of the 3 pieces of wood embedded in the sides, it can be viewed from any angle, and therefore makes an excellent centerpiece candle as well.

Mold Making

Select 3 pieces of wood that have something in common (size, shape, or type of wood) and embed them in the walls of a basic-shape hole which is 8 inches in diameter. For the illustrated candle, I chose 3 pieces of bark. Tamp sand tightly around the edges of the embedded wood to prevent wax from flowing behind it and forming slag on the outside surface (Fig. 8-14). Some wax will always seep around the edges of the wood, but seating the wood well will eliminate some slag cleanup.

It is quite important to make certain that the embedded pieces of wood are positioned widely enough apart across the hole (about 5 inches). Then, when the 3 inch well burns into the candle, the wood will not be exposed. If the wood did jut into the well, the flame could ignite it and start a fire.

Sculpting

Cleaning slag from the embedded bark is a time-consuming task that will test your patience. First, with a tool only, scrape off as much slag as possible. Remove the remaining slag with a torch and brush, being careful not to scorch the wood. I left a matte finish on the surface of the bark so that it would look natural. Carve out patterns that resemble the pieces of wood, and then texture the surface. I chose a dapple-texture to give the surface a convincing bark appearance (Fig. 8-15).

The 3 piece Bark Bowl Candle is as elegant as any driftwood candle you'll ever make.

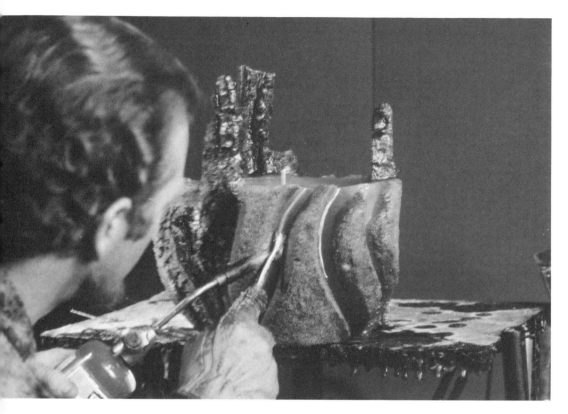

8-15 The Bark Bowl—sculpting

CHAPTER 9

specific shell and stone candles

Shell candles differ from driftwood candles in that their molds require deep undercutting in the seat and in that, as a more delicate material, they need more care in handling. You must never lift a shell candle by the shell or it will separate, and you must take great care when touching the torch flame to the shell or you will crack it.

THE CONCH

Mold Making

As with a driftwood mold, a shell mold evolves from the shape of the shell itself. Because of the conch's shape, a triangular mold evolved (Fig. 9-1). At each of the 3 corners, I then gouged out a 3 fingered scoop of sand. These scooped out areas were to become pods, or feet, and make a tripod candle base.

Be sure to undercut the seat beneath the conch, and to reset the shell. These procedures assure a strong cohesive bond between the shell and the wax.

Sculpting

The conch is one of the most beautiful shell gifts from the sea, and the most appropriate carving pattern for its sandcast candle base is that which comes out of your hands when your mind is pondering the sea.

The first cut I made in the illustrated conch candle (see color insert) sloped from the front top downward in a curve that bisected the front pod. I then cut a complementary line on the other side of the pod, so that a curved "Y" was formed (Fig. 9-2). On the adjoining sides, I repeated the pattern upside down. I then reversed the pattern again on the surface behind the shell. Into each of the "Y" patterns, I now cut a set of grooves parallel to and inside of the first cuts (Fig. 9-3). The sculpted candle now resembled the spiral surface of the conch shell.

9-1   The Conch mold

9-2　The Conch—the first cuts

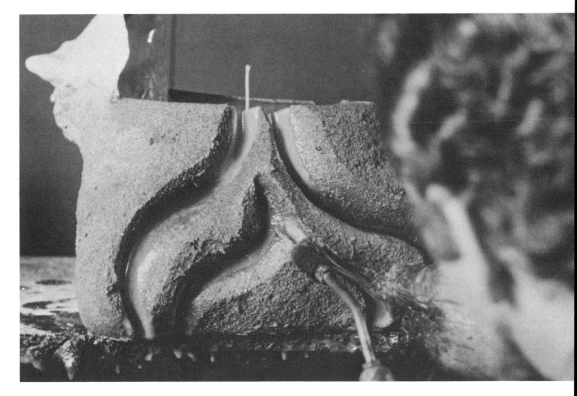

9-3　The Conch—the second cuts

Finally, I removed all of the sand from the small triangular pattern left in the upper, front lip of the candle. Peeling away ribbons of wax, I cut deeply into the grooves of the triangle to make the exposed, pure wax as smooth as the slick, pink surface around the opening of the conch (Fig. 9-4).

THE THREE PIECE ABALONE

Abalone is rarely found whole on the beach. But the more easily found fragments, hopefully weathered, when embedded in the sides of a candle, not only glisten from the outside, but if thin enough, actually transmit light when the candle is burning.

Mold Making

The Abalone mold evolved into an irregular, somewhat pointed, oval shape that closely mirrored the shape of the mounted abalone shell. Note in the illustration of the finished mold that the 2 embedded pieces of abalone are not visible and, that ⅓ of the mounted shell is below the top surface of the mold, to ensure a strong bond with the wax (Fig. 9-5).

Casting the Wax

One special procedure must be followed when casting wax in a mold holding a vertically mounted abalone shell. Because of the deep undercutting required for a strongly bonded cast, the shell is left with a precarious seat that often gives way when the wax is poured. After pouring the wax and resetting the warmed shell, hold the shell in position with one hand. With the other hand, use a pair of tongs to push the shell firmly into the sand behind it and hold it there until it will stay seated.

Sculpting

Cutting the lines is, again, a matter of personal preference and creativity. By now I've described enough sculpting techniques and procedures for you to develop your own patterns for carving and texturing your abalone shell candle. Thus, let it suffice, for the sculpting of The Abalone, for me to simply suggest carving cuts from lines that take cues from the shape of the shell or from a sense of the sea.

9-4
The Conch
—resolving the front

9-5
The Abalone mold

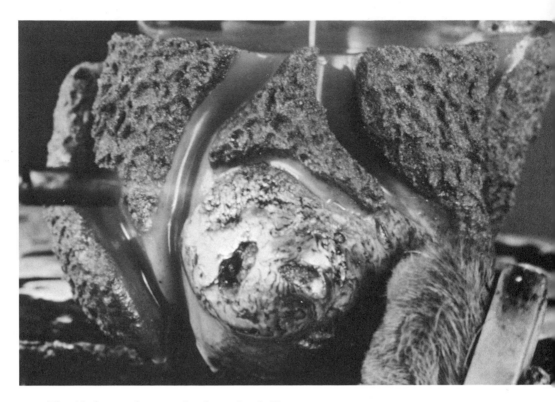

9-6   The Abalone—cleaning slag from the shell

In the illustrated Three Piece Abalone Candle, I carved patterns similar to, though somewhat more curvaceous than, those cut in The Stone Bowl Candle. I selected a dapple-texture, rather than a smooth-texture, in order to complement the shiny, mottled surfaces of the exposed pieces of abalone (see color insert).

Cleaning

Smoke from burning abalone shell (as well as dust when grinding it) is extremely dangerous to inhale. Therefore, when cleaning slag from the exposed, embedded abalone surfaces with a torch, tool, and brush, take extreme care not to burn the abalone (Fig. 9-6). Furthermore, overheating will crack the shell, ruining your almost finished candle.

THE MELON AND STONE

Mold Making

Making The Melon Shell mold was illustrated in Chapter 3 with a specific description of the procedure for undercutting in the mold. Now, into the oval shaped, finished mold we can embed five small stones, positioned so that ⅓ of their mass will be inside the wax, ⅓ will be surrounded by the crust, and the final ⅓ will be exposed on the outside surface of the finished candle (Fig. 9-7). These proportions should be maintained fairly accurately, or else the stones will not be strongly bonded with the wax.

Sculpting

After firing the crust, use a tool and torch to clean the slag and sand from the surfaces, and around the edges, of the stones. Then,

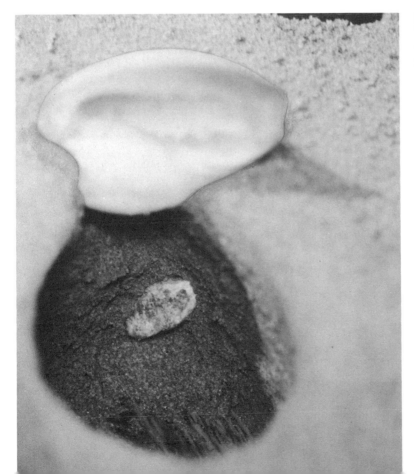

9-7
The Melon and Stone
—stone embedded
in the mold

9-8 The Melon and Stone—deep-grooving

sculpt a pattern around the stones (Fig. 9-8). Take care not to over-heat the stones, for this will cause them to fall out. If this does happen, simply turn the candle on edge, fire the stone's seating, heat and replace the stone, and then let it cool. I again used The Stone Bowl sculpting pattern and, because the stones and melon shell are smooth surfaced, I edged a plain texture on the pattern (see color insert).

As with pieces of driftwood, there is no limit to the types of shells that can be cast in sand candles. The number of possibilities for combining wood, shells, and stones in candles is also unlimited.

With each piece of natural sculpture that you mount in a candle, you will discover new shapes evolving in the mold box and new patterns developing with the torch and tool. Finally, you will explore new materials and discover new kinds of sculptured sandcast candles to make.

102

CHAPTER 10

making the refill

When I first learned that people were not burning my candles I was distressed, and reasonably so, for I had gone to a lot of trouble to learn how to make candles that burned well. My first notion was to provide a piece of wax and a length of wick, with each candle, with directions on how to refill and rewick the candle. But, that idea was too involved, and it would surely create more problems than it solved. When I thought of a small candle that could simply be inserted into the burned-out well, I knew that the problem was solved. All that remained was to develop the process to make the refills.

I began by making molds in sand by hand, but the resultant refills were too irregular. Then, using quart size apple juice jars as impressions for molds, I made refills of consistent size and shape, that fit nicely into the larger candles. The main drawback to this procedure was that each sandcast refill had to be torch-cleaned, which took an inordinate amount of time.

Finally, I thought of using waxed, paper cups as disposable molds for making refills. I discovered that a 10 or 12 ounce cup would make a refill of a size that fit nicely into a burned-out well. The tapered shape of the cup-mold was perfect, as the candle well burns down into a hole of smaller and smaller diameter.

I am presently experimenting with a heat resistant, glass beaker for use as a permanent candle well, but as yet the tests have not proved successful. One of these days the making and the use of the refill will be perfected.

The process described and illustrated in the following pages should be followed carefully. The refill should be made with the same attention and integrity as the candle, for it is one of the main reasons your sculptured candle is permanent. The steps involved in making a refill are pouring the mold, preparing and inserting the wick, tapping, stripping the mold, dipping and filling, torching the top, and trimming the wick. The steps of this process should be followed sequentially and, in most, timing is important.

POURING

Set out the 10 ounce or 12 ounce waxed, paper cups on a level surface and fill them to the brim with wax heated to over 200°. The hotter the wax when poured, the more it contracts when cooled, and the larger the subsequent air pocket. Stripping the cup from the cooled wax is made difficult if the wax was too hot when poured.

WICKING

Preparing the Wick

Hold a length of wicking beside one of the cups and cut it about 1 inch from the top. The wick must be long enough to be grasped with tongs, for dip-filling the refill.

Dip the strand of wick into cool, melted wax, strip off the excess wax with your fingers, and roll the frayed ends into tips. If desired, scent can be added to the wax before dipping the wick into it.

Inserting the Wick

Here, timing is crucial. After the wax has cooled enough to form a ¼ inch thickness on the depressing top surface, take a cold sticker

10-1   inserting the wick in refills

and poke a hole in the exact center of the cup. Then, immediately upon removing the sticker, insert the taut, rod wick into the hole, making sure that it is straight and that it touches the bottom (Fig. 10-1).

If the wick is inserted too long after the sticker has been removed, the wax will have congealed in the hole and the wick will not go clear to the bottom—which is essential if the refill is to burn completely down. If the wick is inserted when the wax has cooled too much, it will not be held strongly enough by the surrounding wax to sustain the weight of the refill when it is picked up by the wick to be dipped.

TAPPING

Three tap, or relief, holes are punched in the top of the refill, after its wick has been inserted, for 2 reasons (Fig. 10-2). First, the tap

holes will strengthen the seating of the inserted wick, and second, they will pierce the air pocket and provide openings for the fill-wax to enter through, during the dipping process.

The 3 relief holes can be made with any tool about ¼ inch in diameter, such as a large nail or screwdriver. The tool that is used must have a larger diameter than the sticker so that the fill wax can easily enter the openings.

STRIPPING

Peel off the cup when the refill has cooled and hardened. If it is not cool enough, handling will dent the soft surface.

DIPPING

Dipping the refill into wax heated to 250° accomplishes two things. Mainly, it fills the air pocket with wax, but it also glazes the outside surface of the refill.

Scent and dye the fill-wax with a teaspoon of liquid scent and a "tip of a teaspoon" of dye the same color as the original candle. Test

106

for color by pouring a few drops of fill-wax on the table and observing its color when it has cooled.

With the toothed tongs, clamp hold of the wick and dip the refill into the 250° wax, leaving it submerged until bubbles stop issuing from the relief holes (Fig. 10-3). Then, remove it and carefully set it down on a level surface.

TORCHING

The wax around the relief holes may not have melted during dipping, and thus there may be lumps on the top surface of the refill. Remove the lumps by torch-fusing the top surface until it is smooth. Avoid setting the wick on fire or melting the wax over the sides.

TRIMMING

The wick in the refill should be trimmed to the same height as the wick in the sculptured sandcast candle, ½ inch measured from the top surface, no more, no less.

10-3
dip-filling
a refill

CHAPTER 11

candle care

All of the love, labor, and integrity imaginable can go into making a beautiful, sculptured sandcast candle, but if it is not properly and lovingly cared for, sooner or later it will go kaput.

THE FIRST 100 HOURS

A candle made from 154°-156° melt-point paraffin and a large-size, wire wick will burn out a well measuring 3 to 4 inches in diameter and 5 to 6 inches deep, in about 100 hours. These first 100 hours are the most important. If the candle is initially placed in a draft, the swaying flame will burn a lopsided well. Even though it will probably still contain a refill, the imperfect shape will detract from the candle's appearance. If the flame is blown-out rather than dipped-out, the wick will smolder and gradually burn down to an unlightable nubbin.

If the original well is not allowed to burn far enough down, or if the original wick was not inserted deeply enough when safety-wicked, the refill will not sit inside the well, and the well will ultimately fill up with wax. Finally, if, when extinguishing the candle, the wick is ever lost, or left "unfished," in the well of hardening wax, it will drown and the candle will be kaput.

THE FIRST YEAR

On one occasion, while I was sculpting on the mall at the Fresno Fashion Fair, a man bought a driftwood candle and said that he intended to burn it every night for 45 minutes and wanted enough refills to last for 1 year.

I figured that for 45 minutes of burning each night, for 365 nights, he would need about 300 hours of candlelight. If the well burned for its reputed 100 hours, and if the refills were good for 50 to 75 hours apiece, he would need 3 refills. He took four refills and a wick-dipper® and, after a moment's instruction, bade me farewell.

By sheer coincidence, I was invited to return to the mall exactly 1 year later. During my stay, the man reappeared and informed me that he had burned his candle 45 minutes every night, without fail, for the past year, had burned out the well and 3 of the refills, and the night before had inserted the fourth refill. He used the candle, he revealed, to focus his attention in meditation, and no one else in his family was allowed to burn it. He had, as he put it, staked a claim on it, it was his candle, and he wanted another year's supply of refills.

The gentleman-meditator obviously got pleasure from burning his candle and so he naturally took care of it. He also, I might add, had listened attentively when I instructed him in the use of the wick-dipper® and the insertion of the refill.

THE WICK-DIPPER®

To eliminate the frequent problems of losing a wick by drowning, and of extinguishing a candle with an internal well (by using match-ends, twigs, and bent paper clips), Jack Belier, a metal sculptor, and I collaborated to design and make a small tool.

The small-rod tool was designed with one end shaped in an "L" fashion so that it can be used to push a burning wick into a pool of wax, to extinguish the flame, and then be used to hook the wick and raise it out of the wax, for easy relighting (Fig. 11-1). Belier devel-

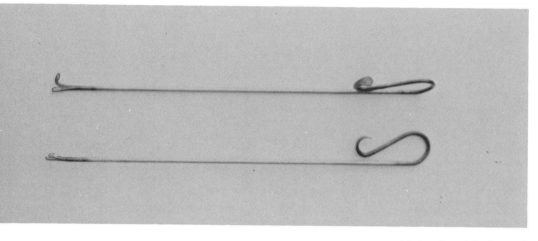

oped a match-holder in the wick-dipper® by sawing a thin groove at the base of the "L." A match can be inserted in this groove and lowered into a deep well to light a candle. The handle end of the wick-dipper® was made in the shape of a shepherd's staff, so that it can be hung when not in use.

EXTINGUISHING THE CANDLE

The wick-dipper® method of extinguishing a candle has several advantages. Drowning the flame in its pool of wax keeps the wick from smoldering away to a kaput-destined nubbin. Thus, not only is the wick preserved, but the noxious odor which rises from a smoking cotton wick is eliminated. In addition, dipping the wick saturates it with wax again and facilitates relighting.

To extinguish a candle with a wick-dipper®, simply push the burning wick into the pool of wax beneath it. Then, hook the "L" under the bent wick and raise it out of the pool, making sure that the wick is straight, and in the center of the well. Straightening and centering the wick are essential. If the wick is left crooked, the flame will not be as large as it should be. If the straightened wick is not centered, it will either burn a hole through the wall, ruining the candle, or melt down too much wax from the walls, flooding the well and drowning the wick. If, upon relighting a candle, you find the wick to be either crooked or uncentered, do not bend it until a pool of wax has remelted, for a cold, charred wick will easily break off.

110

INSERTING THE REFILL

After a candle has been burning for 100 hours or so, its well should be 5 to 6 inches deep. At this point, because of safety-wicking, the wick should be about ready to keel over. Insert the refill either just before, or immediately after, the burning wick falls and extinguishes itself. While the wax in the well is still warm and soft, turn and seat the refill firmly into the bottom. The top of the refill should be flush with, or 1 or 2 inches below, the top surface of the candle (Fig. 11-2). The refill should never sit above the top surface, so be sure that the well is 5 to 6 inches deep before you insert the 4 inch tall refill.

The refill gives the candle a quality of imperfect permanence, which is a far cry from perfect permanence, but is a considerable improvement over a candle with only one wick's life. Although the refill provides the candle with a more functional and longer life, please regard your sculptured sandcast candle as an imperfect, man-hand-made thing of limited permanence. Therefore, the more care you give your candle the longer it will burn and the more glowing light it will bring into your life.

11-2   candle with a refill inserted

CHAPTER 12

candles and candle holders

A CANDLE HOLDER MAKER

One day, while scrounging around in a Topanga Canyon funk shop in search of a new wax-pouring pitcher, I happened upon some sculptured candle holders made from scrap tire chains and other metal objects. I asked for the name of the artist, and a few days later I met Jack Belier. During the next 4 years, we collaborated to develop holders large enough to contain permanent-size sculptured candles. Belier has designed and made candle holders for tables, walls, and ceilings.

A true artist, Belier makes everything he needs from junk and scrap metal, and he never repeats a design. Each holder is a one-of-a-kind, original work. For me, molding and sculpting a different candle for each holder has been a constant source of inspiration.

112

Although I can't describe how Belier makes his candle holders, I can tell you how to make candles destined for holders, and how to fuse the candle and holder together. I hope that this chapter will stimulate you to make holders for your sculptured sandcast candles.

MAKING HOLDER CANDLES

The Mold

The basic-shape mold makes the most suitable candle for most holders. A plump, bowl-shaped mold is also effective when sculpted for a holder, but remember to make the bottom diameter small enough to fit into the base of the holder.

Fitting

Before sculpting the candle, place it in the holder and check it for size. If it is too large, use the torch and scraper to remove some of the sand-crust from around the bottom of the candle. Once fitted, the candle is ready to sculpt.

Sculpting

The holder is as important to the holder candle as the driftwood is to the driftwood candle. Therefore, when sculpting a holder candle, carve and texture the patterns to harmonize with the form and surface of the candle holder.

Fusing

When the candle is fitted and sculpted, torch-heat a pile of slag drippings from beneath the finish table. Spoon this sand and wax, lava-hot goo into the candle holder base and then fire it until it is bubbling, smoking hot. Now, hold the sculpted candle over the holder's base, and torch-melt the bottom, letting the drippings fall into the base. Then, insert, position, and seat the candle, and make sure that it is level. After the base cools, wipe off the excess sand and wax.

CHAIN AND DRIFTWOOD CANDLE HOLDERS

One of Belier's most original designs, the chain and driftwood candle holder illustrates an elegant combination of sand and wax, metal and wood. When sculpting a candle for a chain and driftwood holder, I take my cues from the wood and let the carving patterns develop from there (see color insert).

WALL CANDLE HOLDERS

The pictured wall holders illustrate the use of different kinds of wood as the basis for fixtures. Each produces a different effect when mounted with a burning sculptured candle.

The lighted candle in the grape root holder casts a fascinating gnarled shadow on the wall (Fig. 12-1). The long, tapered piece of weathered redwood comes quietly alive, with the gracious fusion of holder and sculptured candle (Fig. 12-2). The mirrored redwood holder reflects the candle flame, thus doubling the candlelight (see color insert).

SITTING CANDLE HOLDERS

The lantern, by Belier, is sculptured from sheet metal stock and brazed in a dapple, flame pattern (Fig. 12-3). The tripod holder, by

12-1
grape root
candle holder

114

12-2
weathered redwood
candle holder

12-3
the lantern

James Hunolt, is made of pieces of rough-cut steel, welded together (see color insert).

HANGING CANDLE HOLDERS

One of the most medieval looking of Belier's fixtures, the chandelier suspends 5 candles from ring and chains, and has an electric lamp hanging from the center (Fig. 12-4). For a chandelier, it is important to make the candles as similar as possible in shape, as well as weight. When mounting candles into a hanging fixture, check the level of the fixture after the candles have been fused into the base, and add or remove hot mortar to balance it.

From braided thongs to macrame, almost any material that will support a 10 to 15 pound weight can be made into a hanging candle holder. I, personally, prefer latigo leather, for its strength and nature seem to best complement a sculptured candle.

Designed by Dewey Dewitt and handcrafted by Marshall Whitmore, the illustrated leather strap holders are made with 3 thin strips of latigo riveted together at the bottom (Fig. 12-5). A brass ring at the top serves as a hanger, and another ring makes a cinch for the straps.

Whatever holder you choose to suspend your candle, make certain that the candle is level when burning and that it has been safety-wicked at least 2 inches from the bottom. Then, the hanging candle will burn evenly and will not burn through its bottom.

12-4   the chandelier

12-5
candles in
hanging holders

CHAPTER 13

supplies and suppliers

A printer friend of mine, in Los Angeles, once told me that he had never disclosed the names of his suppliers to anyone and he advised me to do the same. I've never fully understood his advice, but I doubt that he would be offended if I disclosed them only once.

WAX

As mentioned in Chapter 2, do whatever needs doing to obtain a source for 154°-156° melt-point, highly-refined paraffin. The highest quality brand I've found, so far, is made by Standard Oil of California. Shop around before buying wax, and begin with at least a 110 pound carton (10 eleven pound slabs). Purchasing wax by the carton is cheaper than purchasing it by the slab. You'll use up 110 pounds of wax in 8 to 12 candles.

My source of wax for the Big Sur Coast-Monterey Peninsula area is:

Salinas Valley Wax Paper Company
1111 Abott Street
Salinas, California 93901

Perhaps the best place for you to begin searching for a source of wax in your locale is in the yellow pages under "Petroleum Products Distributors."

SAND

Almost any sand will work for casting and sculpting, but some types do work better than others. Experiment with the varieties found in your area, and you'll discover which is the most suitable. Avoid using commercially sold sand which has been colored or washed, as it doesn't make a well-bonded crust, and buying it deprives you of the pleasure of digging in the earth with your hands.

WICK

Size "large" wire wick (60-44-18, 2 amp) should be used. It is most readily available in hobby shops or other stores that carry candle supplies. Get the exact type and size recommended and don't skimp on the quality. Buy a few yards if you plan to make only a few candles, but buy a spool if you'll be making quite a few.

I purchase wire wick by the pound, direct from the manufacturer. He asked me not to list him as a source for small quantities of wicking, so he referred me to a mail-order wick supplier who will send a price list upon request:

The Deer Creek Wicks
P.O. Box 8934
Cincinnati, Ohio 45208

DYE

High quality, paraffin-soluble, powder dyes should be used in making sculptured candles. Again, my supplier is the manufacturer, and he requires a $50.00 minimum order—which is enough dye to color several thousand candles. Don't expect a reply to orders of smaller quantities. The address is:

Keystone-Ingham Corporation
13844 Struickmann Road
Cerretos, California 90701

For the small quantities of dye you will probably need, you will find a sufficient selection of colors, at any hobby shop. As with wicking, buy only the best dyes available.

SCENT

Use only paraffin-soluble liquid scent, and use it in small quantities. An ounce will give a nice fragrance to a dozen candles. My supplier is the manufacturer, and he also won't fill orders of less than $50.00, but for reference:

Felton International
2242 Purdue Avenue
Los Angeles, California 90064

For your purposes, you can buy scent where you buy your wick and dye—from whichever local supplier carries the highest quality materials.

FELT PADS

Self-adhesive felt pads, for the bottoms of your candles, are an optional, but thoughtful, finishing touch. If you cannot find them locally and you think you will have use for at least 2,000, 1 inch felt pads, you can order from the following supplier:

Deccofelt Corporation
527 South Vermont Avenue
Glendora, California 91740

PROPANE TORCH

I have used the Sears Craftsman torch head and tank refills because they are as good as, if not better than, the more widely publicized torches. Also, the head and refill tank, as well as the replacement orifices, are less expensive than other brands.

If you use a disposable propane tank, watch for loss leader sales at hardware and department stores. The torch and tank system I recommend is a refillable tank system which is available from propane distributors.

CARVING TOOL

Marples Wood Carving Tools, crafted from Sheffield Steel, are the best tools I have found for sculpting sandcast wax. The manufacturer's address is:

Marples and Sons, Ltd.
Hibernia Works
Sheffield WI 3 TQ, England

The correct tool to use is called a "#26 spoon-bit gouge." It comes in two widths, small (¼ inch) and large (½ inch). If possible, you should have at least one of each size to begin with.

After contacting my supplier, the local Marples Tool distributor, I learned that Marples Wood Carving Tools are not readily available in all areas. Therefore, if you cannot locate either a Marples spoon-bit gouge, or a suitable substitute, write to me and I will supply you with the tool. Send $5.00 for each Marples tool, and specify large or small:

K the Candler
Coast Gallery
Big Sur, California 93920

DRIFTWOOD AND SHELLS

Your local supplier for driftwood and shells is the nearest sea, desert, forest, or stream. As mentioned before, avoid buying these materials. Explore for and discover your own driftwood, shells, and stones because a walk with nature is where making these candles all begins. There, on the floor of the earth, are an infinite number of exquisite natural sculptures waiting to be discovered and placed in the glowing light of a sculptured sandcast candle.

index

GARY KOEPPEL

I was born in a small farming and logging community in Oregon's Willamette Valley. From my father, a dental technician, and my mother, a ceramist, I learned how to work with my hands. My childhood summers were spent at Heceta Head Lighthouse, on the rugged Oregon Coast, with my great aunt and uncle. There, I learned to love and respect the sea and its many gifts.

I graduated from Oregon State University in 1959, in pre-dentistry, and then attended the University of Oregon Dental School. I withdrew during the first year when I came to the realization that what was in people's minds was of greater interest to me than what was in their mouths. So, I went to Portland State University for my bachelor of arts degree. From there, I went to The State University of Iowa's Writer's Workshop on a creative writing fellowship, and received a Master of Fine Arts in 1963.

After teaching writing and experimental courses at The State University of Iowa, The University of Puerto Rico, and Portland State University, I resigned from college teaching and moved to Southern California. For the next 4 years, I explored the medium of wax and sand. My experiments and discoveries developed into the innovation of a new art form—sculptured sandcast candles.

Now, living in Big Sur and sculpting candles in my studio at the Coast Gallery, my life has come full cycle. I am still learning by exploration and discovery, teaching by example, and writing about my experiences.